FIGHTING FOR
CHANGE
IN YOUR
SCHOOL

ASCD MEMBER BOOK

Many ASCD members received this book as a
member benefit upon its initial release.

Learn more at: **www.ascd.org/memberbooks**

Harvey Alvy

FIGHTING FOR
CHANGE
IN YOUR
SCHOOL

How to Avoid Fads and Focus on Substance

Alexandria, Virginia USA

1703 N. Beauregard St. • Alexandria, VA 22311-1714 USA
Phone: 800-933-2723 or 703-578-9600 • Fax: 703-575-5400
Website: www.ascd.org • E-mail: member@ascd.org
Author guidelines: www.ascd.org/write

Deborah S. Delisle, *Executive Director;* Robert D. Clouse, *Managing Director, Digital Content & Publications;* Stefani Roth, *Publisher;* Genny Ostertag, *Director, Content Acquisitions;* Julie Houtz, *Director, Book Editing & Production;* Liz Wegner, *Editor;* Melissa Johnston, *Senior Graphic Designer;* Mike Kalyan, *Director, Production Services;* Cynthia Stock, *Typesetter;* Mike Podgorny, *Senior Production Specialist*

PAPERBACK ISBN: 978-1-4166-2413-4   ASCD product #117007
PDF E-BOOK ISBN: 978-1-4166-2415-8; see Books in Print for other formats.
Quantity discounts are available: e-mail programteam@ascd.org or call 800-933-2723, ext. 5773, or 703-575-5773. For desk copies, go to www.ascd.org/deskcopy.

ASCD Member Book No. F17-9 (Aug. 2017 P). ASCD Member Books mail to Premium (P), Select (S), and Institutional Plus (I+) members on this schedule: Jan, PSI+; Feb, P; Apr, PSI+; May, P; Jul, PSI+; Aug, P; Sep, PSI+; Nov, PSI+; Dec, P. For current details on membership, see www.ascd.org/membership.

Library of Congress Cataloging-in-Publication Data

Names: Alvy, Harvey B., author.
Title: Fighting for change in your school : how to avoid fads and focus on
    substance / Harvey Alvy.
Description: Alexandria, Virginia : ASCD, [2017] | Includes bibliographical
    references and index.
Identifiers: LCCN 2017016603 (print) | LCCN 2017029929 (ebook) | ISBN
    9781416624158 (PDF) | ISBN 9781416624134 (pbk.)
Subjects: LCSH: School improvement programs.
Classification: LCC LB2822.8 (ebook) | LCC LB2822.8 .A62 2017 (print) | DDC
    371.2/07—dc23
LC record available at https://lccn.loc.gov/2017016603

----
26 25 24 23 22 21 20 19 18 17   1 2 3 4 5 6 7 8 9 10 11 12

To Bonnie and Rebecca

FIGHTING FOR
CHANGE IN YOUR SCHOOL

How to Avoid Fads and Focus on Substance

1. Pursuing Reforms of Substance: The Time Is Now _____ 1

2. The Narrative Trap and Building a Collaborative
   Learning Community _____ 17

3. Overpromising and Overloading and Effectively Using Human,
   Fiscal, and Material Resources _____ 53

4. Minimizing the Enormous Difficulty of Implementation and
   Respecting the Change Process _____ 79

5. Eyes Off the Prize and Sustaining a Coherent School
   Mission and Vision _____ 104

6. Historical Amnesia and Embracing Timeless and Eclectic
   Teaching Practices _____ 119

7. The Business "Solution" and Championing and
   Empowering the Underserved _____ 138

8. Conclusions: A Dialogue Among 3 Teachers and
   10 Takeaways to Support Reforms of Substance _____ 164

Appendix A: Protocols for Discussions on Red Flags
   and Guidelines _____ 180

Appendix B: Questions to Promote Collaborative Discussions
   of Red Flags and Guidelines _____ 186

Appendix C: A List of Educational Initiatives, Ideas, Practices,
   and Trends from the Past 30-Plus Years _____ 195

Appendix D: Perennial and Recent Education-Related
   Either/Or Dilemmas_____ 199

Appendix E: The 15 Principles to Support Reforms
   of Substance _____ 201

References _____ 203

Index_____ 213

About the Author _____ 221

Acknowledgments _____ 223

Pursuing Reforms of Substance: The Time Is Now

You can use an eraser on the drafting table or
a sledgehammer on the construction site.

Frank Lloyd Wright

Principle #1: If a reformer or vendor tells you, "All the research supports 'New Reform X,' and the reform will be easy to implement in your school or classroom," it's time to head for the hills.

The main goal of this book is to help teachers and administrators select and promote meaningful and lasting reforms *that improve teaching and learning* by avoiding harmful educational fads. Addressing this goal is an extremely difficult challenge but also an urgent matter with high stakes, as it directly affects student achievement, teacher success, fiscal and resource accountability, and the public's confidence in schools. No one can predict with certainty whether a proposed innovative reform or a reintroduced classical practice will lead to classroom success—it is hard to read the tea leaves—but we at least know that we can't keep doing what we're doing. We need to be more thoughtful in how we make decisions.

Addressing the main goal of this book begins with figuring out why educators have implemented so many unproductive reforms. In Chapters 2 through 7, we'll examine six "red flags" that have inhibited reform as well as six attendant guidelines for how to avoid each one. The guidelines include research findings, recommendations, examples, and strategies for advancing successful reform efforts. The main goals of each guideline are to disrupt red flags and further reforms of substance.

Collaboration will be critical for reforms to achieve results. Teachers, administrators, parents, community stakeholders, potential reformers, academics, state and federal education officials, consultants, policymakers, and foundation experts can all use the material in this book to effect educational change.

What Is Educational Reform?

Tyack and Cuban (1995) define reforms as "planned efforts to change schools in order to correct perceived social and educational problems" (p. 4). At the same time, they insist that change "is not synonymous with progress. Sometimes preserving good practices in the face of challenges is a major achievement, and sometimes teachers have been wise to resist reforms that violated their professional judgment" (p. 5). Sirotnik (1999) maintains that most reforms are "about whatever is politically fashionable, pendulum-like in popularity, and usually underfunded, lacking in professional development, and short-lived" (pp. 607–608), noting that too many reformers focus on "mandates and accountability schemes" while overlooking context, commitment, and the resources necessary to implement change. Sirotnik contrasts reform with *renewal*, stressing that reforms have a beginning and an end (e.g., teaching leads to students' scores), whereas "renewal is not about a point in time; it is about all points in time—it is about continuous, critical inquiry into current practices and principled innovation that might improve education" (p. 608).

Far too many of today's reforms are outdated and reduce success to little more than test scores. A system that does not thrive on continuous improvement and innovation can't meet the needs of students who will continuously need to reinvent themselves in the future: According to the U.S. Department of Labor, 21st century graduates will experience more than 10 jobs during their lifetime—some of which do not yet exist—compared to the two or three jobs that 20th century workers typically held (Darling-Hammond, 2010).

It is unfortunate that the term *reform* has such a negative connotation for many educators these days—a line of thinking some trace to the U.S. Department of Education's famous 1983 report, *A Nation at Risk: The Imperative for Educational Reform*. There is no reason that the term should continue to be associated with regressive policies that offer few advantages for today's students. Returning to Tyack and Cuban's definition of reform as an undertaking "to correct perceived educational and social problems," we might constitute *reform* to mean stakeholders partnering to address the academic, social, economic, and health inequities that many students face both inside and outside of school. Seen in this way, the links to reforms of the progressive era of the early 20th century related to child labor laws, women's rights, safe factories, and fair business practices become clear (Goodwin, 2013). Put simply, reforms are a positive moral enterprise—collaborative and holistic "barn raisings" that require contributions from educators and community members.

Too often, reforms conceived at the national, state, or district level are not contextually conducive to success in individual classrooms. When top-down efforts are the focus, reforms that begin in a single classroom or school may be overlooked. Consider a scenario in which several teachers in a school professional learning community encounter success using an intervention to improve the reading skills of underserved Title I students—peer coaching in reading groups, perhaps. If the success of this intervention is replicated, it may then spread throughout the school and eventually the district in a bottom-up manner. Small-scale reforms of this sort should be celebrated. Reforms can affect the entire educational system, a single group of students, or any magnitude in between. Change in one class-room or school can have a ripple effect as educators and students share skills with one another and use them in new contexts.

Fads, Enduring Ideas, and Innovations

Frequently, educators feel an urgent, sometimes desperate need to improve teaching and learning *now*. They sometimes feel pressured to make decisions without having all the facts or simply suffer from wishful thinking—*there must be a solution out there!* Fads thrive when educators look for the "quick fix" to help students.

Joel Best (2006), an expert on the psychology of fads, empha-sizes that "institutional fads" in business and education can be very expensive and time-consuming and should never be treated as insig-nificant. According to Best, there are three distinct phases to the life of a fad: (1) the beginning, when it gains popularity; (2) the middle, when it peaks; and (3) the end, when it abruptly diminishes in popu-larity (think of fashionable diets, exercise products, and self-help books, for example).

One major recent contributor to fads is the increasing miniatur-ization of technology. As science quickly advances, each new device is smaller, more powerful, more convenient, and capable of performing more functions—thus rendering its predecessor a passing fad. Educa-tors who implement fads in one school will often want to try them if they move to a new school. They also have a tendency to get emotion-ally involved and think ahead of themselves—*Maybe this intervention will, as promised, finally raise the reading scores of every student in the class! If every other school is doing it, we need to get on board!*

Enduring Ideas

In contrast to fads, *enduring ideas* remain influential over time even if their popularity fades somewhat. In education, one example is the concept of *checking for understanding*—a term originally coined by Madeline Hunter and associated with her lesson design. We may relabel the term (as *feedback,* for example), or slightly modify her lesson plan, but the basic concept of checking for understanding has been institutionalized as a critical reform and teaching strategy (Hattie, 2009; Schmoker, 2011a). Once the practice became widespread and even expected in schools, thousands of teachers who had previously conducted linear lessons regardless of students' levels of understanding found themselves modifying their lessons to better honor student voice.

Reforms will often endure because of their crossover or interdisciplinary appeal. The smartphone is not just an updated telephone; with thousands of apps available, it has the capacity to meet health, leisure, work, family, and social needs. Similarly, in education, Grant Wiggins and Jay McTighe's (1998) Understanding by Design approach is used across disciplines to meet teachers' curricular, instructional, assessment, and professional development needs.

Innovation may be defined as a new and significant revolutionary product or methodological change. Of course, newness does not always translate to better results. It is not an exaggeration to say that billions of dollars have been spent on educational reforms and innovations that proved to be unsuccessful. This needs to end. The literature on educational change is replete with examples of superficial structural changes that well-meaning reformers believed would affect classroom practices but that have had little effect (Elmore, 1995, 2011; Frontier & Rickabaugh, 2014; Fullan, 2011; Payne, 2008; Tyack & Cuban, 1995). Examples include lengthening the school year, changing the governance structure, modifying the high school schedule, exchanging tablets for traditional textbooks, closing underperforming schools, mandating curriculum changes, and implementing high-stakes testing. Fullan (2011) insists that structural changes have missed the target; as he puts it, "The heart of the matter is instructional improvement linked to student learning" (p. 13).

The Dangers of Reform Overload

The number of reforms that teachers have to deal with simultaneously in their classrooms is simply overwhelming—and it's nothing new. When I worked as an administrator and teacher at international schools in Singapore, India, and Israel two decades ago, I would visit the United States each year to attend educational conferences and was always taken aback by the multitude of new front-burner reforms covering such disparate matters as "site-based decision making, inclusion, total quality management, brain-based learning, block scheduling, gender bias, charter schools, teacher empower-ment, leadership renewal, technology, year-round schooling, state and national standards, coping with gangs and violence, administra-tive and teacher accountability, school-to-work transitions, distance learning, increasing foreign-language instruction, ESL immersion and multicultural education" (Alvy, 1996, p. 1). Practitioners admit-ted to me that when they closed their classroom doors, they decided which reforms to implement or discard based on student needs and their personal instructional comfort zones:

> Teachers know, from their experiences, that reformers come and go and there is no "warranty" that a reform will work. . . . [Thus,] if we consider what we already know about good schools—and keep these ideas in the forefront of our thinking—we are less likely to accept reforms (and "fads") that may do more harm than good. (Alvy, 1996, p. 22)

Some really great ideas for reform can get lost in the shuffle when they are not piloted first and when their implementation is not pre-ceded by sound decision making (Hess & McShane, 2014; Schmoker, 2014). For example, the development of state standards seemed like a harmless idea when first proposed by the National Governors Asso-ciation in 2010. At the time, just about everyone agreed that higher national standards would help states and districts develop more rigorous curriculum documents. But almost immediately, while the teachers and students were still becoming acquainted with them, *the standards were linked to state testing initiatives.* The results were pre-dictable: In 2013, New York State decided to test students in grades 3–8 on math and reading standards, and only "31 percent of students passed the exams. . . . [The previous year,] 55 percent passed in read-ing, and 65 percent in math" (Hernández & Gebeloff, 2013).

Educators and parents lose faith in the education system when policymakers carelessly implement reforms without considering their responsibilities to students and teachers. As Charles Payne (2008) notes, "Poor implementation is harmful not just to the particular teachers and students who are immediately involved; *it also undermines the very idea that change is possible*" (italics added; p. 155).

Of course, educators don't have crystal balls and can never know in advance if a particular reform will create meaningful change, but caution minimizes disasters. A driver may be unable to predict all winter roadway obstacles, but he or she would still be wise to travel with chains, a flashlight, sand, and a shovel. Likewise, educators may not know whether a reform will succeed, but making thoughtful piloting decisions, reading relevant research, and talking with practitioners will certainly increase the chances that it will.

Accepting What We Don't Know: A Difficult Place to Begin

School reformers need to take a deep breath and consider what they do and do not know. Too often, they swoop in with "answers" that are incompatible with local contexts. In his book *The Checklist Manifesto* (2010), Atul Gawande reminds us that professional expertise does not guarantee success: "Even the most expert among us can gain from searching out the patterns of mistakes and failures and putting a few checks in place. But will we do it? Are we ready to grab onto the idea? It is far from clear" (p. 158).

Educators must raise difficult issues and ask good questions to help distinguish between enduring initiatives and harmful fads. Gene Carter (2014) reminds us: "We need to get the questions right. That means . . . we have to be careful about developing solutions based on misdiagnosed problems" (p. 8). This is not always a comfortable process—as Levitt and Dubner (2014) note, it is very difficult to admit "*I don't know.* That's a shame, for until you can admit what you don't yet know, it's virtually impossible to learn what you need to" (italics in original; p. 20).

The Long Shadow of *A Nation at Risk*

So: Why do we keep on making the same mistakes, pursuing reforms that do not improve teaching and learning? Let's return to the issue of structural changes that minimally affect student achievement. At the end of 2015, the secretary of education, Arne Duncan, expressed regret that instructional time had been sacrificed at the altar of high-stakes testing:

> I can't tell you how many conversations I'm in with educators who are understandably stressed and concerned about an overemphasis on testing in some places and how much time testing and test prep are taking from instruction. . . . We can and will work with states, districts and educators to help solve it. (Zernike, 2015)

Consider the following example of too hastily implemented structural reforms. In January 2015, New York governor Cuomo "called for test scores to determine 50 percent of a teacher's evaluation" (Taylor, 2015a). By December of that year, the governor had completely reversed his position, advocating instead for a four-year moratorium on using math and reading test scores as a component of evaluation and supporting the revision of state curriculum standards. The governor's reversal was partly related to student boycotts of statewide tests; in some schools, fully 75 percent of students refused to take them (Taylor, 2015a; 2015b).

There is little doubt that these kinds of reversals cause teachers to wonder whom they can trust and how much of a commitment they should make to implementing new initiatives. As Zernike (2015) puts it, "Many teachers have felt whiplash as they rushed to rewrite curriculum based on new standards and new assessments, only to have politicians in many states pull back because of political pressure."

By tracing the origins of the standards, testing, and accountability movements, we can better understand recent reform reversals, such as the changes to the No Child Left Behind Act (NCLB) that resulted in the Every Student Succeeds Act (ESSA; including devolving education responsibilities back to the states). The modern education reform movement in the United States began with the Reagan administration's 1983 publication of *A Nation at Risk: The Imperative for Educational Reform (ANAR)*. The report demonstrated that a president's bully pulpit can be more effective than actual legislation: Using such vivid phrases as "a rising tide of mediocrity" to describe U.S. high schools and suggesting that Americans were committing "unilateral educational disarmament," the report captured the imagination of politicians, educators, and the public. The general feeling was that if standards did not improve in U.S. high schools, the country would lose its economic edge with other nations (Ravitch, 2010).

Fair or not, the report placed U.S. educators in a defensive posture from which they have not yet recovered. *ANAR* created a narrative that U.S. schools were failing and that our economy was going to collapse if something was not done, and fast. The rhetoric and momentum created by *ANAR* eventually led to NCLB, which mandated yearly testing, and then to Race to the Top, which tightened mandates linking state standards, testing, and teacher evaluations. Due to the combination of NCLB and Race to the Top, "states were spending hundreds of millions of dollars each year on test preparation materials; the schools in some districts and states were allocating 20 percent of the school year in preparing for state tests" (Ravitch, 2014, p. 13). Jal Mehta (2015), professor of education at the Harvard Graduate School, maintains that *ANAR* is still the dominant school narrative: "Many of our current policies, and the assumptions that underlie those policies, are attributable in significant part to the way in which the report framed the debate. If the next generation of educators is to forge their own path, they will need to get out from under the long shadow of *A Nation at Risk*" (p. 20). One of the reasons I wrote this book is because I agree wholeheartedly with Mehta's admonition. Because *ANAR* intentionally passed over societal issues that affect school success such as poverty, segregated housing, inadequate health care, socioeconomic status, race, and parental background, the report was deeply flawed (Tomlinson, in Mehta, 2015). Schools cannot be separated from society, nor should they be. The work of school reform is too complex and important to let any one aspect of society off the hook.

Teaching and Learning as Exhilarating and Always Complex Experiences

Few activities in this world are more complex than teaching and learning. Charlotte Danielson is right—"Teaching is rocket science!" (2012). Teachers refine their craft every day. For example, until I read the books *How People Learn* (Bransford, Brown, & Cocking, 2000), and *Visible Learning* (Hattie, 2009), I did not fully understand how to use student feedback—responses, interactions, and conversations—to modify my own real-time teaching decisions. Hattie's observations and honesty about feedback created an aha moment for many practitioners:

> The mistake I was making was seeing feedback as something *teachers provided to students*—they typically did not, although they made claims that they did it all the time.... It was only when I discovered that feedback was most powerful when it is from the *student to the teacher* that I started to understand it better.... Then teaching and learning can be synchronized and powerful.... Feedback to teachers helps make learning visible. (p. 173)

For me, teaching would never be the same after reading Hattie's book. Student feedback would thereafter always determine the direction of the class. My job was to pay attention to that feedback and react appropriately. Focusing on feedback ensures that each day will take a unique intellectual turn, with students bound to raise points that had not previously been considered. These moments are gifts, though they are not without challenge: To keep up with the creativity and intellectual energy of students, teachers must use the feedback to fine-tune the trajectory of each lesson.

When policymakers and others suggest that a few simple strategies can solve classroom problems, they ignore the sheer complexity of teaching and learning. The demands of one classroom may be very different from those of another classroom. Assuming that successful practices in one setting can be transferred easily to another setting or scaled up without difficulty to hundreds of classrooms minimizes the importance of context and challenges. The phrase *it depends* honors the diverse challenges that teachers and schools face.

Three Focuses of School Reform

To illustrate *it depends*, consider these three different potential focuses for effective school reform from the research literature:

1. Social infrastructure. Payne (2008) states that when students are underperforming and faculty morale is low, "the first year or two of any new initiative may be more about rebuilding the social infrastructure than about them actually implementing anything" (p. 174).

2. Teaching, learning, and literacy. Schmoker (2011a) suggests that teachers need to focus on pursuing a "reasonably coherent curriculum (*what* we teach); sound lessons (*how* we teach); and far more purposeful reading and writing in every discipline, or *authentic literacy*"(italics in original; p. 2).

3. Personalization and social-emotional learning. After studying four urban schools in Florida with large populations of English language learners and poor and minority students, Rutledge, Cohen-Vogel, Osborne-Lampkin, and Roberts (2015) concluded that "personalization for academic and social learning, not instructional quality, was what differentiated our higher and lower performing schools" (p. 1084). The researchers were particularly concerned about focusing too much on the instructional core:

> Educational researchers have identified the instructional core—teachers' curricular and instructional activities in the classroom—as the primary activity of schools. [Other studies] draw our attention toward elements of schooling that are arguably of equal importance to the instructional core, namely, social emotional learning (SEL) and its role in student success. They underscore that learning in schools is a social process, in which both adults and students benefit from environments that cultivate and encourage their emotional well-being. (pp. 1060–1061)

Optimism is warranted about the impact of the social-emotional learning findings. The 2015 ESSA allows for an indicator of student success beyond test scores. This change is firmly supported by ASCD (2015a): "Standardized test scores alone should never be used to evaluate students, educators, or schools. . . . [U]se nonacademic factors [and] use multiple measures of performance." Clearly, there is more than one pathway to school reform; "what works" is complicated— and we still have trouble implementing successful practices at scale. Berliner and Glass (2015) offer an optimistic reflection: "We might despair in the face of this reality [the combination of inputs, outputs, and variables in educational research]. Or we might, instead, feel privileged that we work in a field that is more complex, and thus more challenging, than physics or rocket science."

Leadership and Promoting Reforms That Work

Particularly since the 1990s, teacher leaders and principals have been pressured to address countless new reforms in schools. Because leaders want to make a difference, they face the difficult task of prioritizing and navigating the introduction and implementation of "the latest" practices. They ask: Is this the right reform for this time and place? Will it influence student success? Will underserved students and students in poverty benefit or suffer? Should we put the initiative on the back burner or drop it? Interestingly, the most recent iteration of the National Policy Board for Educational Administration's (2015) standards for school principals addresses the issue of enduring ideas over fads in Standard 10 on "School Improvement":

> (f) Assess and develop the capacity of staff to *assess the value and applicability of emerging educational trends* and the findings of research for the school and its improvement. (italics added; p. 18)

The Action Checklists following the Guidelines sections in Chapters 2–7, the protocols in Appendix A, and the questions for collaboration in Appendix B are intended precisely for this purpose.

Three Big Ideas to Keep Our Eyes on the Prize of Substantive Reform

The following three big ideas will help educators prioritize their decisions when facing countless initiatives they're asked to consider implementing in the classroom.

Big Idea #1: Provide opportunities for all students. The fundamental reason for public schools is to provide every student with an equal opportunity to learn. Unfortunately, too many schools remain segregated, underfunded, and poorly staffed, making it difficult to achieve this goal. Educators need to ask, *Would I want this reform in my own child's classroom? Will the initiative hurt any population?*

Big Idea #2: Innovate, but have the courage to affirm enduring ideas. Headlines are made by reforms that capture the public imagination. But educators also need to affirm and sustain classical values and approaches: caring about students; nurturing a school community of trust; maintaining high expectations for all students; celebrating diversity and civic values; fostering instructional coherence by aligning curriculum, teaching, assessment, student support, and professional development; and empowering student voices. Having the wisdom to affirm successful traditions as well as promising innovations takes exemplary leadership.

Big Idea #3: Celebrate the importance of courageous questions and honest feedback. "The key to learning is feedback. It is nearly impossible to learn anything without it" (Levitt & Dubner, 2014, p. 34). It is profoundly important to embrace tough questions that pinpoint issues and trigger honest feedback, particularly as it relates to the importance of piloting reforms, intentional professional development, prioritizing financial and instructional resources, technology commitments, timelines for implementation, partnering with the community and businesses, and addressing the needs of underserved students. (The protocols in Appendix A and questions in Appendix B will help educators and other stakeholders to address these issues.)

An Overview of How This Book Is Structured

This book is devoted to helping educators identify *red flags* that signal why fads succeed while also providing *guidelines* to disrupt fads and sustain reforms of substance. Each of the following six chapters examines a different red flag and associated guideline. All 12 red flags and guidelines are interrelated and ought to be considered when pursuing new reforms. (Figure 1 shows how the red flags and guidelines are interrelated.)

FIGURE 1
Sequence of Red Flags and Guidelines in This Book

Chapter	Red Flag	Guideline (Antidote to Red Flag)
2	The Narrative Trap	Building a Collaborative Learning Community
3	Overpromising and Overloading	Effectively Using Human, Fiscal, and Material Resources
4	Minimizing the Enormous Difficulty of Implementation	Respecting the Change Process
5	Eyes Off the Prize	Sustaining a Coherent School Mission and Vision
6	Historical Amnesia	Embracing Timeless and Eclectic Teaching Practices
7	The Business "Solution"	Championing and Empowering the Underserved

Chapters 2–7 also include Success in Action sections that offer practical examples of small- and large-scale reforms that work. The Action Checklists in each of these chapters will help individuals and school teams take thoughtful action to support successful reforms. Chapter 8 includes two main sections: A one-act scenario that incorporates the six red flags and six guidelines and 10 takeaways to help stakeholders engaged in school improvement reforms. Appendixes A and B include protocols and questions to help guide

rich conversations among educators. Appendix C lists reforms, initiatives, practices, and trends that have gained popularity (or notoriety!) over the past 30-plus years. Appendix D includes a list of dilemmas that have been known to cause major conflicts among educators. Individuals and collaborative teams should use the lists in Appendixes C and D as reference points for the protocols and questions in Appendixes A and B. Finally, the 15 principles spread throughout the book are listed together in Appendix E.

A Final Thought

When reading books about education, we expect to encounter new ideas and gain insights to improve performance. However, it is also crucial to revisit familiar ideas that more recent experiences cast in a new light. I hope this book provides you with new insights while affirming what you are already doing well.

Chapter Reflections: Questions and Activities

Please feel free to adapt these questions and activities to meet individual or interactive group goals.

Questions

1. Write the names of two educational reforms that are currently very popular or gaining in popularity. In your opinion, are the reforms *fads* or *enduring ideas*? Do you think the two reforms will affect teaching and learning over the next five years? Ten years? Twenty years? Why? What makes a reform enduring?

2. Think about an educational reform that you've changed your mind about. Why has your opinion changed?

3. What new insights, ahas, or concerns have you gleaned from this chapter?

4. What ideas has this chapter reaffirmed?

5. What additional questions need to be asked?

Interactive Activity: A Historical Perspective:
Is This the Right Time, and Is This the Right Reform?

This activity is appropriate for small or large collaborative groups. The activity includes four possible steps. If a major new reform or initiative is under consideration, use all four steps. However, if engaging in a beginning- or end-of-the-school-year activity for goal setting to determine "where we have been, where we are today, and where we want to go," then only use steps 2 and 3.

1. Describe the proposed new reform. State the primary purpose of the reform and list three to five key elements.

2. List five to seven major reforms that have been adopted in your setting during the previous 10 years. Briefly describe the primary goal of each reform.

3. Review the list from step 2 and consider the following questions:

- What patterns or similar themes do the reforms share?
- Do you think the reforms were/are successful? Why or why not?
- What lessons have you learned from reflecting on the listed reforms? Lessons learned may relate to human, fiscal, and facility resources; testing results; original goals; unexpected consequences; surprises; professional development; students; the community; and timelines.
- Did each initiative align with the district or school mission?
- What else needs to be asked?

4. Now return to the proposed new reform initiative. Based on the reforms reviewed from the previous 10 years consider (a) How can the lessons learned from the historical list be applied to the new initiative? (b) Does the initiative need to be refined? If not, why? If yes, why and how? (c) What else needs to be asked?

The Narrative Trap and Building a Collaborative Learning Community

---

Only when we have many different perspectives do we
have enough information to make good decisions.

Margaret Wheatley

One requisite of good decision making is having sufficient information about the challenge under consideration. However, individuals
entrenched in personal or group narratives are unlikely to sincerely
hear the voices of others or to thoughtfully read research analyses
that contradict their positions. This is not necessarily because they
lack respect for the views of others; in education, it may be because
the *work* of practitioners differs from that of outside reformers
and policymakers. Consider the observations of Stanford professor
David Labaree:

> Teachers focus on what is particular in their own classrooms;
> reformers focus on what is universal across many classrooms.
> Teachers operate in a setting dominated by personal relations;
> reformers operate in a setting dominated by abstract political and
> social aims. . . . Teachers embrace the ambiguity of classroom pro-
> cess and practice; reformers pursue the clarity of tables and graphs.

Teachers put a premium on professional adaptability; reformers put a premium on uniformity of practices and outcomes. (Cuban, 2013, p. 165)

If we only speak with like-minded workmates or friends, we risk creating *polar narratives* that create intellectual and emotional walls around our positions. When polar narratives dominate, sharing ideas and engaging in collaborative dialogue about encouraging research, successful practices, or promising policies are unlikely to occur. Because ideas determine actions, the stakes are very high. Students will succeed or fail depending on our actions. If we truly seek to test the credibility of our positions, we must solicit others' views and honestly weigh the pros and cons.

Building a collaborative learning community can reduce the effects of the "narrative trap" red flag. When community members hold common goals, take responsibility for the success of students, and are trusting and respectful during discussions, entrenched narrative walls come down. Respectful discussions also help build social capital—a critical ingredient in successful school communities. These collaborative ideas will be discussed later in the chapter as guidelines to disrupt the narrative trap and sustain ideas of substance.

The Narrative Trap

> Principle #2: There is a difference between holding beliefs with humility and arrogance. Humility embraces feedback and growth; arrogance embraces neither.

Like everyone else, educators express ideas and embrace practices based on a point of view—a personal or collective narrative that they believe holds the keys to student success. A narrative trap is created when we become prisoners of our own points of view. Though it is important to articulate our strongly held opinions, we must also be sure to candidly reflect on them and to consider the views of others. Put another way, we should surround our narratives with windows rather than walls. The narrative trap is a red flag indicating an unwillingness to hear about ideas with which we disagree or are unfamiliar. It minimizes our ability to engage in a great gift of humankind—the joy of learning new ideas, gaining fresh perspectives, and "recreat[ing] ourselves" (Senge, 1992, p. 14).

In a commencement speech for the New School of New York, Professor Michael A. Cohen (2013) encouraged graduates to closely consider how narratives are used in conversation. He reminded his audience that conventional wisdom and debating points are framed as narratives and advised treating them with skepticism, noting that they may or may not be based on fact. Cohen's points are relevant for educators, who are constantly bombarded with reforms based on questionable narratives. For example, the narrative that all schools are failing and that teachers need to be monitored to ensure they adhere to the curriculum was the basis for high-stakes testing and teacher evaluation mandates central to the No Child Left Behind Act and the Race to the Top initiative.

How Personal Narratives Are Shaped

Among the many factors that shape both individual and collective educational narratives are the following:

- early family home life
- school experiences
- personal and professional characteristics
- experiences and beliefs related to race, gender, religion, social justice, and political issues
- income
- teaching or administrative experiences
- mentor/mentee experiences
- personal and professional role models
- supervisors
- career ladder
- friends
- reading preferences
- travel opportunities

Reflecting on how narratives are formed, Elmore (2011) notes: "I used to think that people's beliefs determined their practices. And now I think that people's practices determine their beliefs" (p. 35). Which is it, the chicken or the egg? (Or could it be both?)

Although the internet provides us with countless opportunities to reflect on different viewpoints, technology writer Allan Martin provides a cautionary note:

> As the web becomes increasingly tailored to the individual, we're more likely than ever to be served personalized content that makes us happy and keeps us clicking. *That happy content is seldom anything that challenges our viewpoint,* and there's a risk that this distorts our view of the wider world outside our browser. (italics added; quoted in Ferriter & Provenzano, 2013, p. 20)

Put another way, the internet is what we might call a *digital narrative trap* in which we select and customize sources of content that confirm our own beliefs.

The World of Narratives: Paradigms and Mental Models

To better understand how we get locked into confining narratives that can shape our beliefs about school improvement, it is important to discuss two concepts that are often associated with shaping beliefs: paradigms and mental models.

1. Paradigms. The term *paradigm* became fashionable with the publication of Thomas Kuhn's seminal 1962 book, *The Structure of Scientific Revolutions.* In it, Kuhn defines paradigms as "*models* from which spring particular coherent traditions of scientific research" (italics added; 1996, pp. 10, 175). Kuhn's models include revolutionary methods, theories, and laws used by scientists to solve puzzles of nature, often upsetting centuries of thought. *Paradigm shifts* (or *disruptions,* in business-speak) imply that an old way of thinking (i.e., old narratives) should be discarded for a new way of thinking. Kuhn suggests that each professional field needs to examine how group goals are determined, how individuals are socialized into groups, and what occurs in the professional community to individuals who change their opinions, deviating from accepted norms and narratives. In some communities, changes of opinion are considered signs of weakness. Discussing the challenges of urban school reforms, Payne (2008) notes that we "have too often been more invested in our paradigms than in solving the problems they address. Progressives—among whom I count myself—are as culpable as conservatives. Each side has a set of cherished beliefs about which they cannot think critically" (p. 192).

2. Mental models. Mental models help us to make sense of and cope with the world of ideas. Senge (1992) famously described mental models as "deeply ingrained assumptions, generalizations, or even pictures or images that influence how we understand the world *and how we take actions*" (italics added; p. 8). By directly linking mental models with actions, Senge underscores the importance of examining narratives to understand how selectively people behave. According to Senge, a drawback of mental models is that they filter out new ideas based on "internal images of how the world works, images that limit us to familiar ways of thinking and acting" (p. 174). Cherry-picking among ideas, selecting research studies that agree with our points of view, and engaging in research studies that consciously or unconsciously look to "prove" a particular hypothesis are all common selective behaviors based on mental models. As Einstein noted, "Our theories determine what we measure" (in Senge, 1992, p. 175).

Mental models can distort reality and the truth to the extent that worldviews are reduced to mere impressions, some accurate and some inaccurate (Davis, 2007; McChrystal, 2015). It is not easy to reverse or minimize the effect of a narrative that captures the public's attention. Consider the criticism of *A Nation at Risk* (U.S. Department of Education, 1983) when it first came out. At the time, Ernest Boyer, head of the Carnegie Foundation, dismissed the report, saying, "What we have is a rising tide of school reports" (in Mehta, 2015, p. 22). Boyer and other critics of the report underestimated the power of the narrative that the U.S. economy might collapse if high schools continued to produce "mediocre" results when compared to other nations. A narrative that sticks becomes a magnet for similar ideas. Mehta (2015) asks two piercing questions that are critical to understanding the enormous influence of *A Nation at Risk* on today's reform efforts: "Of all the reports and commissions on education, why did *A Nation at Risk* have such a seismic impact?" and "Why were critics unable to dislodge the dominant narrative?" (pp. 20–21). Take a moment to reflect on these two questions.

Two Narratives, Always Relevant: Realism and Romanticism

The behavior of education practitioners is often rooted in two basic approaches to teaching and learning: *realism* and *romanticism.* Most educators use elements of both approaches at different times. Whereas realism is based on logic and reason (the head, if you will), romanticism is based on emotions and passion (the heart). Practically everyone makes decisions with both the head and the heart. Discussing the two competing approaches as they flourished among 18th century intellectuals, David Brooks (2015) provides a concise summary of the distinction: "The realists distrusted the self and trusted institutions and customs outside the self; the romantics trusted the self, and distrusted the conventions of the outer world" (p. 244).

As an approach to schooling, realism demands firm accountability measures to make sure students and teachers reach their goals. A basic assumption of the approach is that most students are not self-motivated and thus are unlikely to pursue intellectual goals on their own. Consequently, schools must provide a structured environment to help students reach their academic potential. Realism requires academic standards with a precise curriculum, a fixed scope and sequence for each grade, subject-centered instructional strategies, frequent summative assessments, and firm behavioral expectations. A student PowerPoint presentation called "Five Causes of the Civil War" would represent an assessment assignment that conforms to the approach of realism.

By contrast, romanticism is an approach to human potential that places "emphasis on our inner good" (Brooks, 2015, p. 244). This approach promotes a student-centered curriculum, inquiry teaching, collaborative learning, frequent formative assessments, and personalization. Today's maker movement, with creative, hands-on STEM activities and projects, is rooted in John Dewey's Lab School and is a good example of the romanticism approach.

Ask yourself: How do realism and romanticism relate to your narrative about teaching and learning? How have both approaches shaped your teaching? Which way do you lean? By using realism and romanticism as markers to gauge the origins and flexibility of their positions, practitioners can gain a greater understanding of how to process educational issues.

Seeing Beyond Our Own Narratives

It's a good idea to examine the following five common narratives about U.S. schools and reflect on which ones match our worldviews. Doing this can help crystalize our ideas and values. The five narratives are as follows:

1. The American Dream School
2. Schools as Factories
3. No Excuses
4. Schools Replicate Society
5. Schools as Barn Raising Communities

1. The American Dream School. This narrative tells us that all students can succeed if they work hard enough, regardless of race, religion, national origin, socioeconomic status, or gender. This view can be traced back to the 1840s, Horace Mann, and the Common School ideal. Schools are the great equalizer, transmitting an optimistic, patriotic curriculum that promotes democratic values, the right to rise, and equal treatment. The American Dream narrative accepts that the road will sometimes be difficult and that it may take a while for disadvantaged groups to succeed but also holds firmly that evolution and patience *work*—it's just a matter of pulling oneself up by the bootstraps.

I personally am a product of the American Dream narrative. My parents were the children of immigrants, and our family believed that if we attended school and worked hard, success would follow. When I started teaching in Harlem toward the end of the Civil Rights era in the early 1970s, I thought the American Dream narrative worked for everyone. I believed, naively, that staying in school and earning a high school diploma were only indirectly affected by poverty, poor health care, segregated housing, family struggles, and inequities in the justice system. Embracing the American Dream narrative shielded me from reality and may have made it harder for me to effectively reach some of my students.

2. Schools as Factories. During the early 20th century, Frederick Taylor's philosophy of "scientific management" dominated U.S. business. This way of thinking encouraged distancing managers from workers, using scientific studies to increase worker efficiency, and reinforcing bureaucratic efficiency through detailed employee responsibility charts. This philosophy ignored personal agency, the potential of collaborative groups, and the effects of external forces on the factory. By the 1920s, K–12 administrators adopted the scientific management approach, and it remains popular today. Scientific management reinforced assigning grade levels by age, shuttling students from one teacher to another in secondary schools, differing academic and vocational tracks, and judging students based on machine-scored standardized tests. As Darling-Hammond (2010) notes, scientific management in schools aims to replicate Henry Ford's famous assembly line: "The notion was that one could organize all of the facts needed into a set body of knowledge and divide it up neatly into the 12 years of schooling, doling out the information through graded textbooks and testing it regularly" (p. 4).

Not surprisingly, teacher professional development is anathema to a system that perceives teachers as factory workers. The Schools as Factories narrative promotes high profit margins; merit pay incentives; competition between public and charter schools; the public posting of district, school, and class test results as though they were league tables; and the listing of individual teacher evaluation ratings in newspapers. Some proponents of part- and full-time virtual schools, especially those administered by for-profit education management organizations subscribe to the factory narrative (e.g., delivering curriculum and instruction—the product—via the internet) with public schools and virtual schools competing for students.

3. No Excuses. According to the No Excuses narrative, schools and teachers are failing our students; poverty, deficient health care, and social injustice are unacceptable excuses for that failure; and most educators are incapable of cleaning up the mess. One high-profile proponent of this approach is Michelle Rhee, one-time chancellor of the District of Columbia Public Schools. Ripley (2008) describes her quest as follows:

> Rhee could do something no one has done before: she could prove that low-income urban kids can catch up with kids in the suburbs.... Now, [however,] without proof that cities can revolutionize their worst schools, there is always a fine excuse. Superintendents, parents and teachers in urban school districts lament systemic problems they cannot control: poverty, hunger, violence and negligent parents.

The No Excuses narrative prevails despite decades of work on urban school reform, including such notable endeavors as James Comer's School Development Program and the Effective Schools movement of the 1970s. When Rhee left her post after three years, students had not made significant progress in reading or math, and newly hired teachers were leaving the district at an alarming rate. Moreover, the district suffered amid reports that educators failed to aggressively address widespread adult manipulation of student test scores (Merrow, 2013).

University of California professor Pedro Noguera (2011b) takes a dim view of the No Excuses narrative:

> It's become fashionable for policymakers and reformers to criticize anyone who points to poverty as an obstacle to learning and higher achievement. While it is absolutely the case that poor children need dedicated, passionate, and effective teachers and principals to be successful, there is no evidence that even the best schools can overcome the effects of poverty on their own.... To ignore this reality and make bold assertions that all children can achieve while doing

nothing to address the outside-of-school challenges they face is neither fair nor a sound basis for developing public policy. (pp. 9–10)

Noguera's last point is crucial. Why should any segment of society get a free pass when it comes to helping schools and students succeed? If educators are going to be held accountable for student success (as they should), then why shouldn't families, public and private community-based organizations, philanthropic foundations, religious groups, criminal justice authorities, health care providers, government agencies, and the corporations that drive the economy also be held accountable? As Texas school superintendent John Kuhn (2014) put it, the failure of the community to take responsibility "hints at a profound moral laziness at the heart of reform" (p. 124).

4. Schools Replicate Society. According to the Schools Replicate Society narrative, the purpose of schooling is to mirror the economic and social status quo. The narrative holds that historically underserved communities will remain underserved in education because schools replicate society's injustices and keep poor people voiceless. The privileged classes will continue to thrive in schools that affirm the values and powerful social cues specific to them (such as when teachers compliment students for their dress). In this narrative, "schools serve as tools to keep wealth and power in the hands of the white middle- and upper-class groups" (deMarrais & LeCompte, 1999, p. 12).

As with Schools as Factories, the Schools Replicate Society narrative encourages the use of test scores to sort and place students on academic and nonacademic tracks. Darling-Hammond (2010) stresses how IQ and other intelligence tests were used in the early 20th century to suppress the ambitions of Native Americans and immigrants. Citing Louis Terman from the 1920s, Darling-Hammond reports that 80 percent of tested immigrants were found to be "feeble-minded," suggesting that their children "should be segregated in special classes" (2010, p. 53).

Lest we think that the biases of these two narratives have little present effect, Berliner and Glass (2014b) maintain that high-stakes tests help explain "why low-income and minority students often are underrepresented in gifted and talented programs, and over-represented in special education programs" (p. 235). A particularly destructive aspect of the Schools Replicate Society narrative is that it forecasts a dismal future for underserved children and youth. Using tests to permanently label students as failures "is closely related to the belief that intelligence is somehow fixed and unchanging" (p. 236). Carol Dweck's *Mindset* (2008) is notable for rejecting this idea. In it, she contrasts the *fixed mindset*—"believing that your quali-ties are carved in stone"—with the *growth mindset*—believing "that a person's true potential is unknown" (pp. 6–7). Embracing a growth mindset leads to maintaining high expectations for all students regardless of background. (Proponents of the Schools Replicate Society narrative would likely counter that even if we adopt a growth mindset, we still must overcome the sociological and economic forces that suppress historically underserved students.)

5. Schools as Barn Raising Communities. In a traditional Amish barn raising, men, women, and children work together toward the common goal of building a barn—a symbol of prosper-ity for the community. Barn raisings demonstrate how community projects require the expertise of many different individuals with specialized skills, not to mention their hard work. It also takes lots of collaborative planning with posts and beams prepared in advance and securing tools and other resources. The event symbolizes the mutual obligation that members of the community feel for each other, knowing that their contributions will one day be repaid—not because it's required but because it's the right thing to do. When a barn has been raised, everyone in the community can take pride in the project, and social bonds become stronger. Barn raisings involve glitches, humor, adventure, perseverance, celebration, and, most importantly, memories that will weave their way into the lore and culture of the community.

Is Schools as Barn Raising Communities a realistic narrative? I believe it makes a lot of sense. To begin, there is considerable research supporting the notion that a healthy level of social capital (i.e., networks of fulfilling and productive relationships) exists in successful schools (Fullan, 2011; Hatch, 2013; Leana, 2011; Marx, 2014; Noguera, 2011b; Payne, 2008). Town meetings, local school boards, and neighbors banding together to build schoolhouses are all historical examples of social capital that strengthens a sense of community. In fact, social capital permeates successful schools—it's apparent whenever students mentor one another, take pride in the school sports team, play in the school marching band, attend a school play, help out at a senior center, and so on. Especially in light of the fact that the Every Student Succeeds Act transfers accountability from the federal government to state and local authorities, the Schools as Barn Raising Communities narrative is well suited to present conditions.

Each of the five narratives has positive and negative elements to it. The challenge is to combine the strongest of each in the service of teaching and learning. I personally believe that the Schools as Barn Raising Communities narrative is a good place to start since it raises the bar for everyone and reinforces the notion that we all must contribute to the success of our schools.

Confirmation Bias

It's a simple, unconscious act of bias that we all engage in when reading books or articles about education: We underline or highlight a passage and sometimes make a note if an idea resonates with us. But what if an idea goes against our perspective? Do we make a note of it then? Probably not. As Payne (2008) puts it, "Ideology yields neither to evidence nor to experience" (p. 63). Digging in our heels is quite normal, even admirable in some instances. The problem arises when we refuse to look outside of our ideological framework even in the face of compelling arguments.

According to Kahneman, Lovallo, and Sibony (2011), *confirmation bias* "leads people to ignore evidence that contradicts their preconceived notions" (p. 51). A related concept is *anchoring,* whereby individuals "weigh one piece of information too heavily in making decisions" to firm up a preferred position (p. 51). The authors strongly support group decision making as a means of avoiding either conformation bias or anchoring. Hass, Fischman, and Brewer (2014) see confirmation bias as a filter that we use to "absorb information that adheres to our current view" (p. 27). Citing the dispute over the effectiveness of charter schools, the authors note that "if we currently believe that charter schools . . . are the solution to our educational problems, then positive reports about [them] are more likely to catch our eye and to seem more rigorous and logical than negative reports" (p. 27). Confirmation bias helps us to blame others when reforms fail: For example, if a new reading program isn't working, staunch advocates of the program might suggest that it's the teachers' fault for lacking the skill or will to implement it properly or that administrators are to blame for not providing enough resources.

Stuart Vyse (2005) calls our attention to a type of confirmation bias that is as unfortunate as it is understandable: when families and therapists stick to discredited interventions for developmental disabilities (e.g., autism). Vyse tells the story of "facilitated communication," a process in which therapists support the learners' arms as they write to help them communicate their ideas. Unfortunately, compelling research reveals that the process is fraudulent, with therapists wittingly or unwittingly expressing their own opinions of what they thought the learner wanted to express. Vyse suggests that when figures of authority support interventions that others desperately want to succeed, the interventions are likelier to escape scrutiny. (Indeed, he notes that facilitated communication remains in use after being completely debunked.)

Researchers Are Human, Too

Stanford professor Stephen Davis (2007) notes that "most people (scholars included) . . . tend to pay greater attention to research studies that confirm their deeply held beliefs and assumptions than to studies that challenge their sensibilities" (p. 570). If a long-shot strategy conforms to our beliefs, it's just human nature for us to be predisposed to it. In moments of candor, top scientists note that bias is a reality in the world of research. Nobel Prize–winning physicist

Carl Wieman (2014) notes that researchers often fail "to adequately address [their] inherent biases. *Every researcher in every field has a result he or she wants to see and a belief as to what does and does not matter*" (italics added; p. 194). Relatedly, Kuhn (1996) points out that scientific advances occur when we can no longer ignore challenges to our biases. For example, by the 16th century, it became difficult for astronomers to continue asserting that the earth was the center of the universe given the amount of evidence to the contrary. The Copernican Revolution was a true paradigm shift, a rejection of beliefs that had existed for more than a thousand years—though it also led to a period of crisis, because "the emergence of new theories is generally preceded by a period of pronounced professional insecurity" (pp. 67–68).

In education, it is really hard to shift position when millions of dollars and years of toil by students, teachers, and other stakeholders have gone into supporting it. What usually occurs is a slow evolutionary change. For example, the shift from the mandates of No Child Left Behind and Race to the Top to those of the Every Student Succeeds Act has been an evolving effort by politicians, policymakers, and educators to better meet the needs of students. Some of the more unpopular and unrealistic aspects of the previous era's reform agenda—punishing individual schools through Adequate Yearly Progress, setting unrealistic student expectations, and coupling teacher evaluations to student test scores, to name just three—have been phased out in many states (though eliminating mandated testing in grades 3–8 was probably a bridge too far for those invested in the belief that high-stakes testing works). Over time, maybe Payne's (2008) hope for a reduction of "ideological rigidity" in thinking related to urban school reform will resonate nationally. "Heads bloodied by reality," he notes, "some reformers are now willing to reconsider the purity of their ideas, perhaps giving us a window of time during which a more complex conversation is possible" (p. 9).

The Courage to Change One's Path

When Abraham Lincoln became president in 1861, he was desperate to keep the Union together. Though he had always despised slavery, he was willing to let the institution survive in the South to keep the country united. By the middle of 1862, Lincoln realized that this approach was wrong—that slavery and democracy were mutually exclusive. Although his cabinet and many Union generals disagreed, Lincoln decided to issue the Emancipation Proclamation on January 1, 1863. Today, Lincoln is admired for changing his mind; at the time, however, many thought he was weak (Alvy & Robbins, 2010). It takes courage to break out of a comfortable narrative when the evidence points in another direction.

The Audacity to Fail Forward

Where would we be if doctors were not permitted to conduct clinical trials to advance the fight against cancer? In the world of medicine, "innovators and leaders know that failure is and must be an accepted part of the learning process" (Ferguson, 2013/2014, p. 68). By the same token, successful teachers know that even the best lessons have moments that just don't work. I still cringe thinking back to times when I missed the mark as a teacher. When people say that failure is not an option in education, I wonder: How many years did they teach? Marilyn Ferguson, Executive Director of the Center on Education Policy at George Washington University, insightfully notes that it is particularly difficult for educators to admit failure because we all want students to succeed. But if failure is not an option, the natural consequence is that tests and programs become less demanding for students.

Rejecting Old Narratives and Embracing New Ones

Let's consider three individuals who were able to reject untenable narratives and change their worldviews: Diane Ravitch, Jack Jennings, and Howard Gardner.

Education historian Diane Ravitch famously reassessed her support for accountability measures linked to No Child Left Behind, noting that "when we are certain of our opinions, we run the risk of ignoring any evidence that conflicts with our views" (2010, p. 2). Why did she change her mind? "I found myself surrounded by evidence that the things that I had believed for 20 years were not working," she writes. "So I began to re-examine my own ideological biases and premises, trying not to be dogmatic myself" (Ravitch, Marchant, & David, 2014, p. 170). Ravitch came to believe that both NCLB and Race to the Top minimized the effects of poverty on learning and were too focused on reading and math test preparation. Her new narrative de-emphasizes high-stakes testing and includes a recommitment to a comprehensive, balanced, and coherent approach that supports not only math, reading, and the sciences but also civics, history, literature, the arts, foreign languages, and physical education.

Jack Jennings (2015) was at the center of congressional storms related to education for almost 30 years as the U.S. House of Representatives' principal education expert. Reflecting on his years in Washington, Jennings is pleased that legislation mandating inclusion and special services for students with disabilities was successfully passed but laments the bureaucracy and insufficient funding hindering its implementation. Today, Jennings regrets the role he played in arguing for "targeted funding programs and also the standards/testing/accountability framework" because "progress has not been sufficient and the world is changing at such a fast pace" (p. 46). Jennings now finds fault with both the architects of the original Education and Secondary Education Act, who emphasized money as the key to school improvement, and latter-day reformers who "believed that student academic achievement could be improved by setting high academic standards, using tests to measure attainment of those standards, and holding teachers and schools accountable for poor results. . . . Neither of these two extremes proved to be correct" (p. 45). Jennings's new narrative closely matches legislation enhancing the role of states, minimizing extensive testing, and "focus[ing] on improving classroom teaching and learning" (p. 45).

Over the decades, Howard Gardner (2011) has shifted from "a card-carrying enthusiast of progressive education" (p. 42) to an advocate of educational pluralism. Gardner's moment of truth concerning pluralism took place in China, while observing a 1st grade art class. The students were copying a model over and over again. Gardner thought that the approach was good for skills building but inhibited their creative talents. Yet, when the students were asked to draw an unfamiliar stroller, they were able to do so "with considerable skill" (p. 45). This traditional approach, beginning with skills building rather than creative play, is not endorsed by many in the progressive camp. When Gardner left China, he vowed to no longer "fall on a sword to promulgate progressive education" (p. 47). Gardner's essay also includes a very insightful point that is particularly relevant to pursuing reforms of substance and avoiding fads: He observes that although eclectic teaching and learning strategies make sense, policymakers, because of "training" and "pressures," often reject pluralism in favor of "a single, simple, universal solution" (p. 45). This is problematic, not least because *universal solutions are not context-specific*. Classrooms are idiosyncratic; each one requires a different set of strategies for students to succeed.

The Importance of Hearing Others Out

The great philosopher of science Karl Popper noted that when scientists and philosophers promote their most cherished hypotheses, they are always eager to supply supporting evidence. Popper implored scholars *to seek contrary evidence to evaluate the merit of their theories* (Phillips, 2014). The same goes for educational initiatives: When assessing their merit, educators should always question whether they reflect the school's mission and priorities, conduct a balanced review of research, and consider contextual factors and available resources. For example, the ESSA mandates annual reading and math testing in grades 3–8 but also supports multimetric performance indicators. These indicators should reflect each district's priorities (e.g., tracking chronic absenteeism, access to advanced courses, school climate safety surveys, social-emotional learning). Some educators, reformers, and policymakers are uncomfortable even discussing student success beyond measured achievement tests, so narratives will be tested!

Success in Action: Peace Agreement in Northern Ireland

Former Maine senator and diplomat George Mitchell is credited with successfully engineering the 1998 "Good Friday" peace agreement between Protestants and Catholics in Northern Ireland. A narrative of animosity among the different factions existed for centuries, yet peace somehow was reached. As each side's narrative about the other slowly changed, trust between the factions grew. When asked about the difficulty of bridging the divide among opposing factions, Mitchell had this to say:

> Our minds are built in such a way that we have wide-open receptors for information that is consistent with our prior beliefs. We understand it, we digest it, we recall it. But [with] information that is inconsistent with our prior beliefs we have a tiny opening. We don't take it well. We don't remember it. (2015)

Negotiating the agreement was a monumental accomplishment. The key, according to Mitchell, was "patience and learning to listen to others." How can educators learn to listen and work together and take thoughtful action? A good start is to collaborate. In the section that follows, we'll discuss the importance of building a collaborative learning community to avoid the narrative trap. The Chapter Reference Guide (Figure 2) links the narrative trap red flag with the collaborative learning community guidelines by highlighting key chapter points.

Building a Collaborative Learning Community

> **Principle #3:** Hear and celebrate the diverse voices in the community, then pause, before speaking your mind.

Consider the following statement: "A diverse society, to survive, must vigorously debate issues and listen to the numerous voices of the community." For some, this is a tired declaration of political correctness. Reality, however, tells a different story: Groups that seek a variety of opinions and amplify differences are better at innovating,

FIGURE 2
Chapter Reference Guide: The Narrative Trap and Building a Collaborative Learning Community

	Red Flag: The Narrative Trap	Guideline: Building a Collaborative Learning Community
Definition	Isolation created by ignoring narratives, opinions, data, and feedback contrary to our narrative and beliefs	Respectfully working together as trusting and mutually accountable adults in the school and community focused on common teaching and learning goals to support reforms
Big Ideas	• Narratives limit our ability to objectively judge the quality of a reform. • We tend to seek information that confirms what we already believe.	• Collaborative dialogue with active listening increases the exchange of ideas, knowledge base of educators, and ability to effectively address student needs. • School reform must include the voices of teachers, students, and the community as essential elements of the decision-making process.
Essential Questions	• How are my core beliefs and narratives holding up to the challenges of today's educational issues and reforms? • Which issues and reforms do I find particularly challenging? • What can I do to support different points of view in my school and community?	• If social capital is critical to the success of reforms, how can it be sustained in the school and community? • How can the ideas of successful teachers who prefer to work as "solo artists" be included when weighing reforms?
Drawbacks and Advantages	**Drawbacks:** • Deprives students of learning opportunities beyond educators' belief systems and comfort zones • Minimizes opportunities for educators to grow personally and professionally	**Advantages:** • Reforms are more likely to succeed when teachers are major players in the collaborative decision-making process. • Healthy collaboration welcomes skeptics, as their criticism often includes ideas for improvement.
Examples	• Assuming whole-language reading strategies work for everyone • Measuring student success solely by math and reading test scores	• The Comer Process • Edcamps and unconferences • Authentic professional learning communities

generating options, and coping with complexity (Hill, Brandeau, Truelove, & Lineback, 2014). Hearing diverse opinions and building trust across racial and ethnic lines are key to overcoming biases and creating common values and ideals, but collaborations must also be focused on pressing issues related to student success. In their definition of collaboration, DuFour, DuFour, and Eaker (2008) insist that educators must concentrate on "the things that actually impact student learning" (p. 183), working "together interdependently . . . to improve individual and collective [teacher] goals" (p. 483). These goals relate to student learning, assessing student progress, fine-tuning classroom practices, and providing enrichment for students meeting expectations.

Reporting on a study of more than 1,000 4th and 5th grade teachers, Leana (2011) concludes that "it's easy to get stuck in your own ideology if you are working alone. With collaboration, you are exposed to other teachers' priorities and are better able to incorporate them to broaden your own approach to the classroom" (p. 33). Teachers who broaden their classroom repertoires and become eclectic practitioners—a process that takes years—develop the skills to modify their lessons based on content options and student feedback. When collaboration is valued and binds a community, social capital becomes a powerful force that fuels healthy interactions, builds trust, raises spirits, reinforces cohesion, and fosters pride (Broudieu, in Ballantine & Spade, 2004; Leana, 2011). And when social capital is strong, practitioners are more likely to admit unpopular opinions.

Limiting bias and strengthening social capital are by-products of thoughtful collaboration and conversation—the wisdom of the group. In fact, the quality of conversation in an organization can serve as a barometer of organizational capacity. As Brown and Isaacs (2005) note, conversation "is perhaps the core human capacity for dealing with the tremendous challenges we face" (p. 196).

Collaboration That Works: Trusting Teacher Voices

According to Goodman (1995), traditional reformers too often neglect teacher voices in favor of "restructuring" schools, which has had little effect on teaching and learning. He suggests that teacher conversations need to be "rewired" around collaborative and contextual issues to have an effect. Examples of rewiring include educators grading papers together, developing common strategies to raise student expectations, sharing frustrations, and seeking advice about lessons that aren't working.

Tyack and Cuban (1995) further underscore the importance of collaboration when they encourage potential reformers to "focus on ways to improve instruction from the inside out rather than top down" (p. 134). Teachers, they note, are the "street-level bureaucrats [who] make decisions about pupils that add up over time to de facto policies about instruction . . . translated into practice" (p. 135), so it is with them that change agents must collaborate the most. When teachers hear about new reforms, they tend to reflect on the practicalities: Will this work when I close the classroom door? Will it make my work with students harder or easier? Will I see results?

Collaborative possibilities are diminished through accountability policies that create unwelcome competition among individual teachers (e.g., by publicly displaying class test scores). Such policies "fail to capitalize on the potential of some teachers to improve the performance of other teachers and, therefore, will always be limited, since the benefits of greater expertise will be *concentrated in individual classrooms*" (italics added; Johnson, 2012, p. 116). This is tragic for both new and seasoned teachers: For new teachers, formal or informal mentoring is a critical strategy for overcoming hurdles that too often lead them to quit the profession; for veteran teachers, collaborative conversations can reinvigorate careers, providing the wisdom of experience to colleagues and students (Alvy, 2005).

Working in Concert: Virtual Options, Unconferences, Edcamps, and Job-Alike Sessions

Virtual options. Today's digital age has certainly increased the possibilities for productive collaboration. Networked professional development enables individuals to share and seek educational information through Twitter streams, blogs, podcasts, and crowdsourcing sites. These virtual spaces are particularly valuable for those who might be reluctant to express their views in traditional public spaces (Ferriter & Provenzano, 2013; Marx, 2014). Further, the internet enables educators and community members to quickly organize and advocate for topics of concern; for example, the parents movement to opt out of testing has successfully used social media to rally millions to their cause (Blumenreich & Jaffe-Walter, 2015). A strength and risk with social media sites is that they are personal and idiosyncratic. Many sites are made for sharing opinions—however, when opinions dominate, is truth sacrificed for advocacy?

Success in action: Unconferences and edcamps. Rooted in design and digital thinking, unconferences and edcamps have become extremely popular and creative avenues to improvise, innovate, and test both new and classical educational ideas. As Swanson (2014) notes, edcamp conference "attendees collaboratively determine the schedule of sessions on the morning of the event" (p. 36). Participants network online in advance to agree on topics, venues, and logistical issues. Setting up schedules and topics in the morning is a creative process that affirms the professional skills and expertise of practitioners to organize and present information without months of planning. Among the edcamp topics that Swanson highlights are "Public/Private School Partnerships . . . Privacy and One's Digital DNA, Design Thinking and Innovation, [and] Writing in the Digital Age" (p. 37).

Success in action: Job-alike sessions. Educators who attend job-alike sessions discuss ideas in an informal, brainstorming setting that nurtures rich engagement and practical strategies. One of the most successful initiatives that I implemented with parents at the Singapore American School, the Parent Book Club, was the result of a job-alike session for principals: I learned about the idea from Tonya Porter of the Bangkok American School at an international conference. The job-alike facilitator simply asked us to share our best practical ideas, and Tonya described how she connected with parents by drafting them into a school-sponsored book club to read about and discuss issues related to education. Her idea proved to be a great strategy for developing and strengthening relationships with parents.

Is There Room for the Solo Artist?

Bryk and Schneider (2002) note that efforts to implement collaboration in schools are often obstructed by entrenched norms of teacher autonomy. In O'Keeffe's (2012) view, however, the real problem is too much institutionalized collaboration: He argues that collaboration is a fad that pressures teachers into contrived situations where independent conclusions are unpopular. As he puts it, "Teacher autonomy—or, if you insist, teacher isolation—is a critical safeguard against bad ideology. If there is no longer room for individual thought in education, then there is no longer room for ideas ... [or] for innovation" (p. 58). Maybe the truth is somewhere in between and there are benefits to both autonomy *and* collaboration. To quote Hill and colleagues (2014), "At the heart of innovative problem solving is the need to both unleash individual slices of genius and harness them into collective genius" (p. 12).

Begin with Culture, Not Structure

After conducting a decade of research on social capital and urban schools, Leana (2011) concluded that "we are overselling the role of human capital and innovation from the top, while greatly undervaluing the benefits of social capital and stability at the bottom" (p. 32). Grassroots efforts pay off. Most importantly, Leana stresses the relationship between social capital and student success: "When the relationships among teachers in a school are characterized by high trust and frequent interaction—that is, when social capital is strong—student achievement scores improve" (p. 33). Bryk and Schneider (2002) drew similar conclusions in their three-year study of 12 Chicago schools using the term "relational trust" to describe social capital: "In particular, where high levels of social trust exist, the cooperative efforts necessary for school improvement should be easier to initiate and sustain" (pp. 12–13).

It is important to underscore the fact that schools with high levels of trust and teacher interaction are healthy places to express diverse ideas. In these schools, teachers talk to one another about their teaching strategies, past curriculum decisions, or any issues they may be having. When social capital is robust, teachers are more open-minded about analyzing data that trigger discussions on modifying lessons and more likely to escape from their narrative traps, knowing that the culture provides a support system that will help them recover from failure. Fullan (2011) maintains that teamwork and social cohesion provide the "right drivers" (i.e., leveraged policies and strategies) to successfully implement whole-system reform. He also makes the point that successful teamwork leads to enhanced individual capacity.

Of course, not all schools offer high levels of social capital. Payne (2008) describes struggling and dysfunctional urban schools as places where "an overarching sense of futility and pessimism" exists and "harshness" characterizes how children and adults are treated, where supervisors are "distrusted" and students and teachers are "disengaged" (p. 23). When social capital is nonexistent or low, educators must first work on "rebuilding the social infrastructure" (p. 174). Before introducing new programs or reforms, these struggling schools must build trust and collaborative opportunities for teachers, welcome parents, and offer students all the academic and social support they need. Highlighting this point, Payne shares the following findings of the Wisconsin Center for Education Research: "Structural elements of restructuring have received too much emphasis in many reform proposals, while the need to improve the culture, climate, and interpersonal relationships in schools have received too little attention" (Krause, Seashore-Louis, and Bryk, in Payne, 2008, pp. 61–62). Traditional structural changes are visual and garner attention—a new block schedule, new curriculum standards, a new teacher evaluation system, even a new building. But structural changes rarely affect the social infrastructure—that is, what takes place *after* students and teachers enter classrooms.

Success in Action: A Social Capital Success Story in the Segregated South

When legendary baseball player Willie Mays was a sophomore at Fairfield Industrial High School in Alabama, he wanted to play professional baseball throughout the year, which would have resulted in a lot of absences. E.J. Oliver served as the school principal for 43 years.

> Oliver, a graduate of Tuskegee, was also a progressive educator. His students were taught Negro history long before it became fashionable. He oversaw a wide range of clubs—math, science, drama, debate—and encouraged his best students to travel to Montgomery for academic meets. He celebrated black ambition, including athletics. (Hirsch, 2010, p. 44)

Oliver met with Mays's family and told them that if Willie was going to graduate, he couldn't play professional baseball during the school year. His family accepted the ultimatum, and Mays never missed a day of school to play baseball, graduating in 1950.

Interestingly, and surely significant, Mays's English teacher at Fairfield was Angelina Rice, mother of former secretary of state Condoleezza Rice, who recalled her leveraging of social capital fondly:

> Mother taught English. Her former students remember her as a teacher whom you didn't disobey despite her diminutive stature. She was a stickler for good grammar. She was the coach of the debate team and would enter her students in citywide oratorical contests. She also directed student plays and musicals, gaining a sterling reputation throughout the city for her efforts. (Rice, 2010, p. 23)

Neither Principal Oliver nor Angelina Rice fell for the narrative trap of low expectations for black students that white society had created by segregating students in 17 southern states. Committed to excellence, these educators stressed the importance of black history and expanded the curriculum by teaching debate and pursuing the arts. Imagine a principal remaining in the same school for 43 years. *How many reform efforts fail, in part, because school leaders move on?*

The social capital at Fairfield no doubt made a difference in Willie Mays's Hall of Fame career. If he had dropped out in 1948, would he have advanced down the same historic path? Would Mays have had the capacity to persist when faced with challenges on and off the field? We will never know. But we can say that the values and personal examples of E.J. Oliver and Angelina Rice, fighting for their students, had a profound effect on the ballplayer that some consider the greatest of all time.

Teacher Collaboration

Singapore, Finland, and the Canadian province of Ontario all have exemplary school systems that "provide considerable time for teachers to work collaboratively and learn together" during the regular school day (Darling-Hammond & Rothman, 2015, p. 85). These systems produce effective teachers who feel trusted and respected and enthusiastically remain in the profession for decades. Compared to their peers in other industrial nations, U.S. teachers "have less time to collaborate to improve their work" yet they are working harder and receiving less professional development or feedback from principals (Darling-Hammond, 2014/2015, p. 14). Many new U.S. teachers feel they are unsupported and disrespected—a major reason that about one-third of them leave the profession within five years (Darling-Hammond & Rothman, 2015). Citing a Consortium on Chicago School Research study of more than 100 schools with chronic teacher turnover, Johnson (2012) notes that teachers were more likely to stay if they worked in schools "where teachers collaborated, school administrators were supportive, parents were engaged, and the learning environment for students was safe and orderly. They left schools where teachers remained isolated in their classrooms and resisted schoolwide initiatives" (p. 115). Collegial support is an immeasurable morale-booster that can help teachers with tremendous potential from giving up before their talent blossoms. (Conversely, support can also help convince a teacher that teaching is just too difficult a profession to pursue.)

The link between collaborative schools and student achievement has been a mainstay of educational research for more than 25 years (see Bryk & Schneider, 2002; Newmann & Wehlage, 1995; Rosenholtz, 1989). Progress continues as more educators recognize the benefits of collaboration. Consider the findings of a recent study of 9,000 teachers in 336 Miami-Dade County public schools where collaborative teacher work and professional learning communities have become the norm:

> About 85% of teachers now identify as being a part of a "team or group of colleagues that works together on instruction" and report that collaboration in these teams is quite extensive and helpful. . . . Our results also suggest that these instructional collaborations benefit students. *Student achievement gains are greater in schools with stronger collaborative environments and in classrooms of teachers who are stronger collaborators.* (italics added; Ronfeldt, Owens-Farmer, McQueen, & Grissom, 2015, pp. 511–512)

Cuban (2013) labels collaborative teacher discussions about work *pedagogical capital* and notes that they are "a scarce resource because isolation is endemic to age-graded schools" (p. 181). Pedagogical capital affirms blended teaching models and rejects the idea that there is one single best way to teach. "Such collaboration comes far closer to achieving good student learning than big-ticket structural reforms such as funding, authorizing charter schools, mayoral control of schools, accountability and testing, and new curricula" (pp. 181–182).

Collaborating with Students, Parents, and the Community

Sonia Nieto (2011) tells the story of how she was transformed as a young teacher after reading Paulo Freire's *Pedagogy of the Oppressed*. She reminds us that Freire "was about standing up *with*, not *for*, those who are powerless in society and working with them to create change. It was a vision of teachers not as missionaries or saviors but as guides and supporters" (p. 133). Nieto was not alone. Freire's message of social justice resonated with millions internationally because it underscored student and parent empowerment to reduce political and educational oppression. The national movement to opt out of testing is an example of parent activism, as are parent protests of school closings (especially in urban communities). Nieto's reflections are a reminder that collaboration should be a liberating exercise among equals. Freire's work admonishes educators to reject the narrative trap that portrays poor and oppressed people as incapable of determining their futures.

The ASCD Whole Child Approach

The ASCD Whole Child approach was created in 2007 to move "from a focus on narrowly defined academic achievement to one that promotes the long-term development and success of children." ASCD (n.d.) maintains that the "broader community" needs to partner with schools and develop a vision of career and citizenship success "in a global environment" for students. Epstein (2007) notes that in schools with high parental involvement, "students earn higher grades in English and math, improve their reading and writing skills, complete more course credit, set higher aspirations, have better attendance, come to class more prepared to learn, and have fewer behavioral problems" (p. 18). Moreover, teachers who grasp the importance of relationships are better able to "teach content to diverse students in ways that effectively support the learning process" (Darling-Hammond, 2010, pp. 161–162). Johnson (2013) likewise argues that collaborative partnerships are essential: "Unless teachers, parents, students and community members become allies and partners in the mission of improving schools, the United States will likely stumble in its efforts to build a world-class education system" (p. 19).

Collaboration, Personalization, and the Classroom

The ASCD Whole Child approach encourages us to see schools as responsible not only for academics but also for other aspects of child development. Rutledge and colleagues (2015) found that relationships—that is, the social-emotional side of learning—account for the biggest disparities between high- and low-performing schools. In high-performing schools, teachers intentionally work to personalize relationships. Significantly, students noticed when teachers made the extra effort, describing these teachers as "caring" and "involved" (pp. 1069, 1086). The high school principal at one high-performing school stated, "I keep coming back to personalization: Knowing the kids, knowing their background, and creating a sense of family, I think goes a long way" (p. 1069).

When practiced successfully, collaboration becomes part of a school's fabric. Visible evidence of a collaborative culture can be seen in respectful face-to-face interactions among students and adults in classrooms, hallways, during morning and afternoon bus activities, in the office reception areas, and especially in the cafeteria, which often provides opportunities for rich informal student-teacher discussions. And just as it is important for students to feel comfortable in their relationships with teachers and administrators, teachers, too, should feel comfortable with administrators at the school and district levels.

Success in Action: The Comer Process

In the late 1960s, James Comer, a child psychologist at Yale Medical School, began a program partnering schools with parents and the community to improve student lives in and out of school. Since then, the Comer School Development Program, or Comer Process, has been implemented successfully in more than 1,000 schools in 26 states and abroad. From the start, Comer recognized the importance of initiating collaborative holistic local programs involving teachers, students, parents, and the community that addressed child development, academic expectations, social capital, and psychological and emotional needs. The Comer Process succeeds because the school improvement plans are homegrown, based on "professional collaboration, community building, and cooperation," rather than rooted in government mandates (Timar in Ravitch, 2014, p. 61).

The Comer Process connects the school and community with three interactive social and structural decision-making networks that make up what Comer calls the "Basic Framework":

- **A school planning and management team** creates the comprehensive school plan, sets goals, and coordinates activities with administrators, teachers, parents, and support staff.
- **A student and staff support team** focuses on social conditions and relationships, outside resources, and prevention programs; this team includes the principal and key mental health staff.
- **A parent team** develops activities to support academic and social programs with parents and families. (Select parent members also serve on the school planning and management team.)

Three "Guiding Principles" steer the work of each team:

1. No-Fault Problem Solving—Maintains the focus on problem solving rather than placing blame

2. Consensus Decision Making—Through dialogue and understanding, builds consensus about what is good for children and adolescents

3. Collaboration—Encourages the principal and teams to work together (http://medicine.yale.edu/childstudy/comer/about/works.aspx)

Staff development based on the school plan and assessment are essential features of the Comer Process. Reporting on several Comer schools in Chicago, Payne (2008) was impressed with how quickly parents became engaged: They helped on playgrounds, patrolled hallways, served as classroom aides, and assisted with lunchroom duties. Some parents even helped with classroom supervision while teachers were engaged in professional development. Schools that previously had a maximum of 10 involved parents could now call on up to 100 of them. "It was very clear the children felt good about having their parents involved," writes Payne. "We were caught off guard by how much the parents themselves were affected by their own participation. They took pride in what they were doing and developed more confidence in their own abilities" (p. 202).

The Broader, Bolder Approach Policy Initiative

The University of California's Pedro Noguera (2011b) advocates for the "Broader, Bolder Approach" (BBA) to education, a national policy initiative based on an "ecological framework" that supports combining social services with a school's developmental and academic program. The BBA philosophy matches the Comer Process as both efforts accept that school success depends on the full support and involvement of the greater community. The Harlem Children's Zone and the Children's Aid Society Community Schools are both BBA coalition partners. Noguera contrasts the BBA policies with those of reformers who prefer the "schools-alone strategy" that has wasted billions of dollars "revamping school curriculum, retraining teachers, introducing new technology, and making schools smaller . . . [without having] had the desired effect on academic and developmental outcomes for children" (pp. 11–13).

A Disappointing Effort, but the Work
Continues in Newark Public Schools

In her book *The Prize* (2015a), Dale Russakoff offers an in-depth analysis of what can go wrong when traditional reformers fail to initially collaborate with community stakeholders. She writes of reform efforts in the Newark, New Jersey, Public Schools that used millions of dollars donated by Facebook's Mark Zuckerberg to transform schools using a top-down model (to the tune of about $20 million in consultant fees). The reforms aimed to run the schools more like businesses, introducing more charters and firing ineffective teachers (Russakoff, 2015b). The reform effort was introduced on the *Oprah Winfrey Show* on September 24, 2010, to great fanfare, with Zuckerberg, Newark mayor Cory Booker, and New Jersey governor Chris Christie all appearing to extol its virtues. Unfortunately, Newark community members had not been consulted about the plan before the televised announcement.

Although Russakoff believes that the reform effort had some success, she concludes that it did not have a major effect on student performance overall and caused tremendous anger in Newark.

Among other problems, the failure of would-be reformers to consult and collaborate with the community about the merits of a "universal enrollment" plan that allowed students to attend the school of their choice caused confusion and challenged neighborhood cohesion. According to Russakoff,

> The reformers never really tried to have a conversation with the people of Newark. Their target audience was always somewhere else, beyond the people whose children and grandchildren desperately needed to learn and compete for the future. . . . There was less focus on Newark as its own complex ecosystem that reformers needed to understand before trying to save it . . . and almost five years later, there was at least as much rancor as reform. (2015a, pp. 209–210)

Russakoff (2015a) shares the thoughts of Howard Fuller, the former superintendent of Milwaukee Public Schools. Fuller regretted the approach he had taken as a school reformer: "I think a lot of us education reformers . . . have been too arrogant," he said. "Why do you think you can just get in a room and make decisions for a community of people" (p. 210)? Arrogance pretty much guarantees the absence of a healthy exchange of ideas. In the case of Newark, those most affected by the decisions had been excluded from their decision-making role. Certainly the Newark reform effort was well intended, but intentions are not enough; communities must be respected. (On a positive note, Zuckerberg and his wife Priscilla Chan may have learned important lessons from the Newark experience. They are now working on a project that involves a school partnering with a community health center and other organizations to "[create] a web of support for students with the greatest need, beginning in early childhood" [p. 214].)

A LESSON LEARNED

Success in Action: A Ballpoint Pen Can Herd Cats

When Steve Barone introduced himself as the facilitator of the Singapore American School strategic planning initiative, I looked around the room and knew he would have considerable difficulty getting the group to collaborate and agree on major points. Our group of more than 100 individuals from all over the world represented teachers, administrators, counselors, classified staff, parents, middle and high school students, and community stakeholders. With 100 strong-willed personalities, all passionate about education, I wondered how Steve would gain consensus.

He opened the session with a simple visual prompt that has remained with me. Steve positioned himself in the middle of the room (we were sitting in a circle) and held his hand up high, with a ballpoint pen extended from his fingertips. He said, "Whenever someone shares an idea during our sessions, suspend the idea from the person and let it stand alone as on the tip of this pen. Separate the idea from the individual." It was an ingenious suggestion and helped all of us realize that our ideas, and the ideas of others, were much more important than who we were. Following Steve's initial comments, egos vanished and the group got down to business. After several months of fruitful, creative, and stimulating collaborative dialogue, we produced a first-rate strategic plan.

☑ Action Checklist to Avoid Narrative Traps and Promote Collaboration

When considering reform initiatives during collaboration:

_____ 1. Ensure that discussions never lose sight of the critical question: How will the initiative directly affect teaching and learning?

_____ 2. Ensure enough collaborative time to prioritize the most pressing needs for all students and for specific targeted groups.

_____ 3. Provide opportunities for staff to reflect on their own narrative traps and reflect on the implications.

_____ 4. Discuss the consequences of confirmation bias and the importance of institutional collaboration that values research and contextual experiences.

_____ 5. Use strategies that promote collaboration with key stakeholders in the school and community. Create inviting forums that welcome and celebrate input from diverse groups.

_____ 6. Foster professional learning community behaviors focusing on student goals, teacher accountability to students and each other, professional development activities, goal timelines, and evaluating student outcomes.

_____ 7. Advocate for teachers to play a major role alongside administrators as decision makers in the reform process.

_____ 8. Encourage skeptics of the proposed reform to express their views.

_____ 9. Promote social capital by assessing how the school culture can strengthen the bonds between school and community.

Chapter Reflections: Questions and Activities

Please feel free to adapt these questions and activities to meet individual or interactive group goals.

Questions

1. Create a brief list of three or four prevailing narratives about schools in your state, district, or school. What assumptions do these narratives make?

2. What narratives about education do you personally embrace? Feel free to review the five narratives discussed in the chapter or to create your own. What core beliefs have shaped your narratives?

3. Why are the issues of confirmation bias and how individuals courageously revised their narratives important to consider when pursuing educational reforms?

4. You are responsible for creating an agenda to stimulate a rich conversation on school reform. What are your top three discussion items? Why are these items critical?

5. Reflect on your own creative thinking process. Do the ideas flow better within a collaborative setting, do you prefer to work alone, or are you equally comfortable with both approaches? What are the reasons for your preference?

6. Based on your experiences with social capital, what conditions should be fostered in schools to make teachers, parents, and community stakeholders feel welcome as equal partners?

7. Based on reading this chapter, what new insights, ahas, or concerns do you have?

8. What beliefs has this chapter reaffirmed?

9. What additional questions need to be asked?

Interactive Activities

Activity: Embracing the Other Point of View

1. In groups of two or more, discuss two or three narratives that define how schools do or should work. Make sure to include enough

narratives so that each group member opposes at least one of them. For example, one group of four may only need to select two narratives to meet the criteria, while another group of three might need three separate ones. Feel free to create narratives that were not addressed in the chapter.

2. Select a narrative that you oppose and embrace it for the duration of the activity. Take a few minutes to write down the core beliefs behind it. Describe how the narrative might be successfully implemented in a school setting.

3. Share your narrative ideas with other group members.

4. Discuss any takeaways.

Activity: What Are the Characteristics of a Collaborative Group or Community?

This activity is adapted from Marx (2014):

1. In small groups, discuss and have a group member record five to seven characteristics of an effective collaborative group based on your experiences and ideas in this chapter.

2. Each group member individually ranks the characteristics in order of importance.

3. Members compare rankings and discuss major differences of opinion.

4. Optional: Reflect privately on the characteristics discussed and on how your school or district fares on each.

5. Discuss any takeaways.

Overpromising and Overloading and Effectively Using Human, Fiscal, and Material Resources

Eisenhower warned the country against belief in quick fixes. Americans, he said, should never believe that "some spectacular and costly action could become the miraculous solution to all current difficulties."

David Brooks

This chapter addresses two challenges that are so interrelated it is best to address them as one red flag: overpromising and overloading. Overpromising is the unrealistic and sometimes harmful guarantee of initiative success promoted by legions of reformers, policymakers, vendors, program developers, politicians, pundits, and, yes, educators. Overloading is when too many initiatives spin simultaneously in a teacher's world. A heightened understanding of these two phenomena can help educators to minimize their effects.

If reforms are based on fads, and if too many are taken on at once, everyone suffers: Students are hurt, teachers are less likely to take future risks and more likely to lose confidence in the administrators and policymakers who promoted the reforms, precious time is lost, and billions of dollars are wasted. As Best (2006) cautions, the quick fix is tempting, "but the best way to become fad-proof is to insist on persuasive evidence and be skeptical about astonishing claims." To progress, we need to thoughtfully promote both innovative and timeless success strategies. Righting the ship will be difficult. The brutal reality of making good decisions, prioritizing, and working with limited resources must be addressed. To begin, the school mission and vision are the first overpromise and overload deterrents. But staying smart is not easy. Marketing experts, vendors, and policymakers (often ideologues) know how to make a sales pitch to captivate their customers—customers who desire a miracle product or strategy now. Thus, the second major chapter section will provide guidelines, tips, and advice to disrupt the overpromise and overload red flag to help districts and schools support initiatives of substance.

Overpromising and Overloading

Principle #4: Today's quick fix is tomorrow's problem.

Tyack and Cuban (1995) note that "policy talk about educational reform has been replete with extravagant claims for innovations that flickered and faded. . . . [I]t has often led to disillusionment among teachers and to public cynicism" (p. 10). Phrases related to overpromising include *quick-fix, teacher-proof, guaranteed results,* and *turnkey answers.* Educational history is filled with promised panaceas that discount the depth of the education challenge (Paul & Elder, 2007).

Reforms come with such frequency that initiative overload is normal. A newly hired superintendent of a modest-size school district informed me that a review of the district's recent history revealed 70 currently active reform initiatives; reducing that number is now a top priority. Too rarely do we ask, What should we reduce or eliminate when a new reform is proposed and implemented? Consider the dilemma of Heather Austin, the principal at Mount Pleasant High School in Delaware. Herold (2015c) describes the whiteboard behind her desk displaying 19 shapes surrounding a circle depicting a Mount Pleasant student. Each shape represents a different initiative the school is pursuing, from the state's teacher evaluation scheme to online tests related to state standards.

Bryk (2015) introduces the term *solutionitis* to describe the propensity of educators "to implement a policy or programmatic change before fully understanding the exact problem to be solved" (p. 468). Bryk maintains that the pressure to find immediate answers leads to groupthink and insufficient examination of alternative solutions. Failing to consider context when seeking solutions is another common misstep. For example, many reformers perceive breaking up large high schools as a solution to several of the challenges faced by urban school districts. In one district, doing this may indeed lead to increased personalization; in another, however, it may disrupt the positive relations that already exist and reduce the number of advanced placement (AP) course offerings. Payne (2008) contends that when "good ideas are understood out of context, when they are reduced to The Solution, they become part of the problem" (pp. 5–6).

Tyack and Cuban (1995) compare the advocacy of for-profit schools as cures for all ills to Thomas Edison's claim that radios would replace teachers and that motion pictures would transform the classroom. Overpromising is especially unfortunate and discouraging when educators, parents, and clinicians are desperately looking for solutions for students with disabilities. Schreibman (2005) describes the typical sequence of events that give special education fads credibility:

1. Because a known cure for the disability does not exist (e.g., autism), people search for miracle interventions and seize on promising stories.

2. When the miracle intervention is discovered, it is publicized and promoted in the media, capturing public interest.

3. The intervention's popularity is sustained by continued intense media coverage and anecdotal stories of success.

Schreibman has little tolerance for false promises and warns teachers and parents: Buyer beware. As she puts it, "If there is no supporting research to back the purported effectiveness [of an intervention], then my advice is to hold onto your wallet and walk away" (p. 227).

Ensuring That Resources Are What They Say They Are

A common overpromising strategy is to capitalize on a fashionable educational movement, initiative, catchphrase, or acronym (e.g., blended learning, coding, NCLB, PLC, CCSS, PARCC, ESSA). To illustrate, after the National Governors Association rolled out the Common Core State Standards (CCSS) in 2010, numerous books came out with CCSS in the title—but how many of them were truly about standards in any meaningful way? The annual textbook market is a $9 billion business, and the Thomas B. Fordham Institute suggests that transitioning to new math and language arts standards costs districts across the United States between $5 and $12 billion over three years (Cavanagh, 2014a). Of course, if standards didn't exist, billions would still be spent on curriculum and assessment material, instructional and technological resources, and professional development initiatives. Standards or no standards, educators need to prioritize when purchasing resources and eliminate items that do not address essential teaching and learning needs (Cavanagh, 2014a; Herold & Molnar, 2014).

William Schmidt, a professor of statistics at Michigan State University, worked with a team that examined 35 different K–8 textbooks series and more than 700 textbooks and warned districts, "Don't spend your money until [materials] arrive that actually fully line up" (Herold & Molnar, 2014). Similarly, the University of Southern California's Morgan Polikoff studied 4th grade math textbooks and concluded that publishers cover content satisfactorily but "systematically overemphasize procedures and memorization and underemphasize more conceptual skills" (2015, p. 1206). Polikoff cautions that if teachers depend only on math texts, "they will systematically fail to teach the advanced cognitive-demand levels called for by the standards" (p. 1207). Clearly, both Schmidt and Polikoff are advising adoption committees, teachers, curriculum directors, principals, and superintendents to examine and pilot hardcover and digital texts and programs, regardless of publishers' promises about standards or assessments alignment fidelity.

Overpromising also includes the misuse or overuse of terminology (e.g., professional learning communities [PLCs], project-based learning, blended learning), which can diminish the unique promise of a program or practice. For example, DuFour (2004) argues that the term *PLC* "has been used so ubiquitously that it is in danger of losing all meaning" (p. 6). DuFour insists that PLC advocates must emphasize three "big ideas" that distinguish PLCs from other collaborative professional development programs: "ensuring that students learn . . . , [supporting] a culture of collaboration . . . , [and emphasizing] a focus on results" (pp. 6–11).

The Dismaying Consequences of Overpromising

In Bryk's (2015) analysis of education reform efforts, he laments the failure of change agents to foresee the consequences of overpromising: "The incidences of test score cheating accelerated, and select students were ignored as accountability schemes directed attention to some students but not others" (p. 468). Bryk views these detrimental effects as the "unintended consequences" of failing to thoughtfully consider implementation difficulties.

When success is gauged solely through test scores, it is reasonable to assume that teachers will narrow the curriculum and use strategies to match outcomes that they know will be tested. As social scientist Donald T. Campbell has said, "The more any quantitative social indicator is used for social decision making, the more subject it will be to corruption pressures and . . . distort[ing] and corrupt[ing] the social processes it is intended to monitor" (in Cuban, 2013, pp. 88–89). Campbell suggested that achievement tests, in particular, were susceptible to corruption. Campbell's observations do not excuse uncovered cheating scandals, but his sobering analysis reminds us that when promises are made, and the public expects success based on test scores, results should be viewed with a degree of skepticism. Relatedly, Calfee (2014) holds that accountability measures instituted during the NCLB era determined "what is taught, how it is taught, and how it is assessed" (p. 1): "Reading was portrayed as a set of basic skills, to be trained during the early school years by direct instruction" (p. 2). Of course, in reality, it is critical for teachers to entertain a variety of instructional reading strategies depending on student needs, with direct instruction serving as one of many possibilities.

Initiative Overloading: It's Hard to Say No

The United States has approximately 15,000 school boards, none of which are bound to follow a national curriculum, particular instructional approach, or technology plan. The wisdom of this approach is often debated. In the United States, just about anyone with leverage can influence the direction of schools at the expense of mission coherence. Elmore (2011) laments the role that policymakers play in a system "run amok":

> There is no political discipline among elected officials and their advisers. To policymakers, every idea about what schools should be doing is as credible as every other idea, and any new idea that can command a political constituency can be used as an excuse for telling schools to do something. (pp. 34–35)

Elmore believes we need to focus on the important work of practitioners and heed their advice over that of policymakers. The role of administrators is to serve teachers and students, after all.

Schmoker highlights how overloading and careless initiative planning occurs by noting that once "state standard documents were launched and hardened into law, it was discovered that it would take about 20 years to teach all of the skills and topics contained in them" (2014, p. 28). Schools work hard to accommodate the demands of parents, students, and other stakeholders, which can naturally lead to overloading. Nehring (2007) refers to this tendency as "the Politics of Appeasement" and uses as an example a rural school determined to accommodate parents' requests for more than one foreign language class. In striving to make such accommodations, schools must consider teacher credentials, faculty loads, and budgetary limitations, among other things.

It's easy to suggest that educators should be more selective about the reforms they choose to pursue, but they are often caught between a rock and a hard place. Some reforms are mandated by the federal or state government (e.g., high-stakes testing and state standards); others simply feel like mandates. For example, to remain globally competitive, U.S. educators are actively involved with the STEM movement promoting science, technology, engineering, and math education. Art advocates believe that STEM is narrowly focused and should be STEAM; and reading and writing advocates are equally firm that STEAM should be STREAM. Bryk stresses that teachers' work has become increasingly complex as they are overloaded by demands to meet the needs of at-risk students while "the list of new educational ideas continues to grow at a dizzying pace" (2015, p. 470). Bryk cautions that the knowledge explosion in education does not guarantee successful outcomes. Drawing an analogy to the world of medicine, he quotes Dr. Atul Gawande: "In surgery, you couldn't have people who are more specialized, and you couldn't have people who are better trained. Yet we still see unconscionable levels of death and disability that could be avoided" (p. 470). More reforms do not guarantee progress.

A major reason for reform overload is a failure to coordinate initiatives. Bryk (2015) suggests coordination must begin with understanding systems and "how all of this joins productively together" to address complex issues (pp. 470, 476). It is imperative that educators embrace complexity, systems, and coherence by aligning instruction, curriculum, assessment, instructional resources, and professional development to the specific needs of their schools.

The Marketing of Programs and Products to Educators

Competition among corporate vendors, product developers, and consultants to win the minds, hearts, and—most importantly—wallets of educators is just as brutal in the education world as it is in the commercial retail world. Billions of dollars are at stake. One of the oldest and most successful marketing strategies is the overpromise. The following list of **10 marketing strategies, slogans, and**

catchphrases used to sell products is worth examining before making any procurement decisions. Consider adding to the list based on your professional experiences.

1. ***Simple to understand*** **and** ***teacher-proof.*** These terms are related to **content** and are meant to assure educators that it is easy to understand how to use the product and that every teacher and student can learn the program. Related advertising catchphrases include *powerfully simple, assessment made easy,* and *simple tools.*

2. ***Easy to implement.*** This approach relates to **process** and assures the smooth implementation of the steps or stages necessary to carry out the program. Related advertising catchphrases include *user-friendly* and *simplifies practice.*

3. ***Provides instant success/results.*** Tactically, this strategy satisfies educators who desire, or are required to provide, evidence of instant success. Related advertising catchphrases include *so fast, immediate impact,* and *accelerated.*

4. ***Use with all groups, anywhere.*** This slogan ignores context and implies that the product in question can be scaled up. Related advertising catchphrases include *reach every student, every class, every day; ensure all will succeed; empower every learner; integrate into any classroom;* and *proven program.*

5. ***Guaranteed to work.*** Related advertising catchphrases include *unstoppable success, most effective practices, most proven, research shows,* and *most powerful research.*

6. ***Proven recipe/secret sauce.*** This type of slogan entices consumers by suggesting that the product is mysterious but perfect and can be revealed only to those who courageously pursue it. Related advertising catchphrases include *the three keys to guaranteed success, the five dimensions that will guarantee unlimited growth, the only program that offers 100 percent success,* and *nine essential skills to meet every student's needs.* Of course, there are many excellent programs that offer "five steps that can lead to success"; but what separates these programs from the *proven recipe or secret sauce* marketing strategies is the 100 percent assurance—the guarantee of success—that leaves no room for the complexity of teaching and learning.

7. *Revolutionary/part of a new wave.* This kind of pitch assures educators that the product is on the cutting edge of education and is used most often to sell technological devices and software. Related advertising catchphrases include *new modes of delivery, reinvent teaching and learning, reimagine digital learning,* and *transform the classroom.*

8. Slogans that incorporate fashionable terms and relabeled practices to match popular jargon (e.g., NCLB ad "renewed" as ESSA). These slogans encourage educators to demonstrate that they are compliant with popular new reforms. Related advertising catchphrases include *CCSS-aligned; flexible, blended, personalized; for the flipped classroom; compatible with mobile devices and laptops;* and *STEM program, growth mindset, brain science.*

9. *All-inclusive.* This slogan promises educators they will not have to depend on other programs or supplemental resources to address any challenges. Related advertising catchphrases include *all-in-one program, definitive program, complete solution,* and *everything you will ever need.*

10. Slogans in the form of endorsements and testimonials. These types of slogans use validating words from practicing educators to assure credibility. Related advertising catchphrases include *five-star program, the gold standard, award-winning, the most trusted, dramatic results, 100 percent success with my class,* and *every assignment I give is completed.*

On a refreshing note, a professional development book advertisement stood out because the author did not overpromise. Modestly the author stated that the guidelines "attempt to show" how to implement the program. Seasoned practitioners might be more inclined to purchase that book as the ad projects trust from an experienced colleague who knows that a book's impact or the success of a professional development program is not guaranteed. There are thousands of first-rate educational products, programs, and services available. But it is imperative for educators to do their homework, vetting products to discern which ones best meet the contextual needs of students, teachers, and schools.

When the Research Agenda Marginalizes Context

Each educational setting includes unique contextual variables. A study may be research-based, but until it is locally piloted, its efficacy for any individual school will remain unknown. At the end of the day, a practitioner is not really interested in how successful an intervention is 500 miles away or with 50,000 students in another country. As Davis (2007) reminds us,

> The problem is that there are no silver bullets. What works in one setting or with a particular group of people will inevitably play out differently (subtly or significantly) in different settings or with different people. Practitioners are wise to examine scientifically based research, but always with the understanding that, in the education business, "one size rarely fits all." (p. 575)

Davis illustrates his point by examining the movement for smaller high schools related to personal attention, achievement, and the impact on urban, suburban, and rural youth. Davis highlighted the findings of a National Association of Secondary School Principals report: "Implementing small learning communities will not, in and of itself, increase student achievement. It may help to do so, but the studies do not provide conclusive evidence of this point" (Quint, in Davis, 2007, p. 573). As a result of compelling data, the Gates Foundation, originally a major financial supporter of the movement, began to temper its support. The lesson is clear: Context cannot be ignored.

A Story of Hubris: Overpromising, Conflict of Interest, and the Reading First Program

Reading First (RF) was a $4 billion federal literacy reform program instituted from 2002 to 2008 as part of NCLB. McGill-Franzen (2010) notes that RF advocates sought to "eliminate the reading deficit" among different groups (p. 275). *Eliminating* a challenge is a classic overpromise; unfortunately, a conflict of interest further complicated the challenge. In 2006, the Office of Inspector General, in its Final Inspection Report, stated that government officials and university consultants, both enthusiastic RF supporters, had become so convinced of the merits of direct instruction that they ignored federal restrictions on promoting any particular program in schools. "The ESEA [Elementary and Secondary Education Act] does not advocate any particular reading program, assessment, or other product," read the Office of Inspector General report. "In fact, Section 9527(b) of the ESEA *prohibits* the Department from endorsing, approving, or sanctioning any curriculum" (p. 5). The report concluded that the director of RF selected members of the program's reading panel who shared his preference for direct instruction:

> The Reading First Director took direct action to ensure that a particular approach to reading instruction was represented on the review panel. Direct Instruction (DI) is a model for teaching that requires the use of [the program] Reading Mastery. . . . The Reading First Director personally nominated three individuals who had significant professional connections to DI to serve on the expert review panel. (p. 17)

In the end, a Reading First Impact Study found that the program affected instructional practices, and "teachers did what they were told to do . . . [but the] program impact on reading comprehension was negligible" (Calfee, 2014, p. 5). McGill-Franzen (2010) adds,

> [The] RFIS [Reading First Impact Study] found a significant impact on the amount of instructional time spent on the five NRP [National Reading Panel] essential components—phonemic awareness, phonics, vocabulary, fluency, and comprehension—including a positive and significant impact on decoding in Grade 1. However, there was no significant impact on reading comprehension in Grades 1, 2, or 3. (p. 276)

Here are some takeaways from the RF story for school practitioners:

1. Narrowing teaching options to a single teaching method (e.g., direct instruction) devalues a teacher's capacity to adjust instructional strategies and deprives students from learning a variety of skills.

2. State, district, and school leaders need to ask tough questions related to overpromising and conflicts of interest. Are independent evaluators or special interest supporters providing unbiased research data on a program?

3. We all have our points of view. However, biases regarding reforms and purchasing decisions must be refuted to effectively impact teaching and learning. Cherry-picking data to present to a school district is unacceptable. Even a billion-dollar government program based on scientific research and intended to reform reading instruction can be flawed. To make thoughtful decisions related to school change, educators should always welcome productive skepticism, nurture collaboration, and embrace contrary views.

Maybe optimism and hope explain why educators are so susceptible to overpromises. Educators *want* to believe that the next idea is a silver bullet. Paul and Elder (2007) suggest that educators can't "get off the educational fad rollercoaster" because doing so would mean acknowledging that a panacea doesn't exist (p. 6). Yet it is vital not to yield to promises that fall short. Using common sense and thoughtfully considering decisions forces educators to face the brutal reality that resources are not infinite.

The Chapter Reference Guide (Figure 3) links the overpromise and overload red flag with the guidelines on effectively using human, fiscal, and material resources by highlighting key chapter points.

Effectively Using Human, Fiscal, and Material Resources

> Principle #5: When making decisions about resources, programs, and professional development, always ask: How will this decision affect student learning and teacher success?

It's worth stating at the outset that human, fiscal, and material resources do not all have the same value. Human resources—the people who serve students in the classrooms and beyond—are by far the most important. This seemingly obvious point needs to be made because there are pockets of reformers who think advanced technology, high-stakes tests, and curriculum resources are equally as

FIGURE 3

Chapter Reference Guide: Overpromising and Overloading and Effectively Using Human, Fiscal, and Material Resources

	Red Flag: Overpromising and Overloading	Guideline: Effectively Using Human, Fiscal, and Material Resources
Definition	• Overpromising: unrealistic and sometimes harmful guarantees of reform success • Overloading: tackling too many initiatives simultaneously	Intentionally procuring and using resources to meet the school mission, keeping excellence, equality, and equity in mind
Big Ideas	• Reforms, which are often no more than fads, are promoted without a full understanding of context. • Multiple reforms are initiated without coherence, often sparked by the latest trends or mandates.	• Intentionally supporting new reforms by holistically addressing instructional, curricula, assessment, and professional development needs within fiscal limits • Ensuring that resources do not hurt any segment of the population
Essential Questions	• How does the reform process distinguish between staying on the cutting edge, keeping up with the Joneses, and doing what is best for students? • What is being replaced, modified, or eliminated when new reforms are adopted?	• How are we ensuring that our school mission is the driving force behind decisions to procure resources? • How are we prudently integrating technology with other instructional resources?
Drawbacks and Advantages	**Drawbacks:** • Too hastily yielding to marketing pitches can lead to implementation of ineffective initiatives. • Guaranteeing student success can lead to unethical practices.	**Advantages:** • Procurement decisions guided by the school mission promote coherence and dissuade the selection of fads. • Prudent selection of resources maximizes the possibility of sustaining reforms.
Examples	• Purchasing products simply because they promise to be Common Core State Standards–aligned • Assuming general research findings for an initiative will work in a specific school context without piloting the initiative first	• Strategic plans with delimiters • Using total cost of ownership strategies when procuring technology resources

important. A school district might be fiscally solvent and have an array of impressive resources, but inanimate assets do not guarantee curriculum coherence, engaged students, effective teachers, community support, social capital, or visionary leadership (Grubb, 2009/2010).

Darling-Hammond (2010) quotes Ferguson as noting that "skilled teachers are the most critical of all schooling inputs" (p. 106). And yet, highly experienced skilled teachers are not at all fairly distributed in the United States. The truth is that students with the greatest needs routinely receive the least experienced instructors. Darling-Hammond refers to this inequity problem as the opportunity gap: "the accumulated differences in access to key educational resources—expert teachers, personalized attention, high-quality curriculum opportunities, good educational materials, and plentiful information resources—that support learning at home and at school" (p. 28). Educators cannot close the opportunity gap alone; the community must help. Building trust and networking effectively (i.e., expanding social capital) with public and private agencies is therefore vital (Henig, in Elmore, 2011; Hatch, 2013). District and school networking contacts often involve partnerships with community-based organizations and various other groups, including the following:

- universities and community colleges
- museums
- senior citizen centers
- religious centers
- the League of Women Voters
- hospitals
- health and dental clinics
- sports associations
- homeless shelters
- the Gay, Lesbian, and Straight Education Network
- women's centers
- merchant associations
- YMCA and YWCA
- Boys and Girls Clubs
- scouting organizations
- drug and alcohol rehab centers
- local park and recreation departments
- police, fire, and emergency service personnel
- the U.S. Forest Service
- the National Park Service
- the U.S. Armed Forces
- traditional and internet news media and social networks

Dedicated classified staff, often residents of the local community, may be as important for some students as the classroom teacher. The official job description of a school secretary may not include public relations expert, psychologist, doctor, substitute teacher, or guardian of the school's traditions, but secretaries know that on certain days they assume all these roles. Classified staff are also an important local political force capable of influencing school board, levy, and bond voting. As the late Phil Snowdon, superintendent of the Cheney, Washington, Public Schools said frequently about town constituents, "They are local, vocal, visible, and they vote."

Tying Procurement to the Institution, Not Individuals

Schools in the United States spend more than $3 billion a year on digital content alone (Herold, 2015c). As Grubb (2009/2010) reminds us, "Many district, state, and federal 'reforms' have come and gone, with billions spent and nothing to show for them" (p. 52). This waste of funds often occurs when the failed reform is closely tied to particular staff members and ends up "abandoned by a new principal or superintendent with different priorities" (p. 52). Of course, reforms should not rise or fall solely because they are promoted or initiated by charismatic or powerful individuals. Although it takes determined people to stir up enthusiasm for a new initiative, team decisions, collaboration, and staff development are absolutely crucial if the initiative is to succeed when those people move on. Ideas and institutions must be sound enough to sustain success *after* the most vocal and influential proponents of a reform effort have long departed.

Educational Resource Strategies (ERS), a nonprofit organization dedicated to helping districts make sound fiscal and resource decisions, insists that the most resourceful schools know how to prioritize and "start with a clear vision and instructional model . . . align[ing] all their resources and attention around it" (Calvo & Miles, 2011/2012, p. 19). ERS economists maintain that districts and schools risk allocating funds arbitrarily if they make fiscal decisions without first checking their mission statements and forget that program coherence and prioritizing resources are driven by student needs. ERS has a first-rate website with excellent content, up-to-date examples, and interactive tools for assessing resource use, prioritizing which resources are most important, exploring budgeting options, visioning the future, leveraging teacher talent, assessing professional development, and refining student schedules (see www.erstrategies.org).

Focused Professional Development for Using Resources Successfully

According to Grubb (2009/2010), one major reason for reform failure is that districts too often invest in resources without providing teachers with the necessary professional development to successfully use them. This is a formula for failure. Daccord and Reich

---

A LESSON LEARNED

Success in Action: Supporting the Mission Takes Commitment

As noted in the previous chapter, I was fortunate to help craft a comprehensive strategic plan at the Singapore American School. The final plan included seven strategies with accompanying goals. Committing our resources wisely was an essential component of the plan. As a pie-in-the-sky thinker, seeing how the plan was grounded in reality was a good lesson for me. The plan's success was contingent on three related factors, or "strategic delimiters":

1. Any new initiative would be considered *only* if it was consistent with and contributed to the school's mission (our coherence check).
2. A new initiative would be implemented *only* if effective staff development—with fiscal support—could be put into practice.
3. Each strategy included a timeline with an assessment component to evaluate its success.

In short, the strategic plan taught us to be thoughtful and accountable when taking on new reforms.

(2015), managers of the school technology consultancy EdTech Teacher, constantly see districts spending considerable money on resources while devoting minimal funds to in-service training. They bluntly conclude that "if investments in technology aren't paired with investments in teacher capacity, change is unlikely" (p. 22).

Schmoker (2015) maintains that providing funding for professional development addresses only one aspect of the problem. Too often, he argues, professional development is unfocused or centered on "unproven fads" (p. 19). To restore trust in professional development, Schmoker recommends directing "all professional development time . . . to a severely reduced number of powerful and proven practices" (p. 18). He stresses "a clear, coherent curriculum" and thoughtful lessons infused with Madeline Hunter's key tenets: "a clear purpose . . . in digestible steps . . . [with] checks for understanding . . . [allowing teachers] to adjust, reteach, or clarify throughout the lesson" (p. 19). Schmoker also stresses that professional development should address *the specific needs of students.*

Guidelines for Improving the Resource Allocation Process

Effectively allocating resources to students and teachers begins with a collaborative procurement effort between the central office and school personnel. The proliferation of technological resources in particular demands the involvement of end users such as students and teachers who will be manipulating and customizing the tools for classroom use (Johnson, 2015; Martin & Pines, 2015). The former chancellor of New York City Public Schools, Harold Levy, warns us that "too many school districts buy ed-tech products on the basis of good marketing rather than careful analysis—the way a child is attracted to the hot toy of the Christmas season" (2016, p. 23).

Each state and school district has established procurement procedures with detailed forms to ensure legal compliance, monitor expenses, and track delivery and distribution of resources. However, procedures do not guarantee that students will *actually benefit* from the process—only the educators involved can determine whether high-quality products are ordered for students. The following **guidelines** are intended to ensure that procurement promotes student success.

1. Begin with mission and coherence. All procurement decisions need to align with a district's mission regarding its obligation to students, focusing on classroom interactions with teachers. A district budget should therefore be viewed as a financial plan to address student needs. A budget is not a framework to save money; it is a plan to spend money wisely.

Coherence obligates us to ask how a proposed resource purchase aligns with what we are already doing in school. When districts innovate, establishing coherence may not be so easy—which is fine as long as everyone agrees on what to do.

2. Foster collaboration between schools and the central office. There are benefits to making procurement decisions centrally as well as locally. At the district level, staff can receive volume-based purchasing discounts and work with other districts on cooperative purchases. District-level IT directors are also often well versed in each school's technical requirements. At the same time, involving end users in the process is critical. Teachers who are involved in selecting instructional resources, professional development programs, and books feel affirmed as professionals and are much more likely to use the products.

3. Pilot implementation. Piloting is a primary strategy to check overpromising. Flanigan (2013) cites two good examples of piloting the use of resources before committing to them. In Henry County, Virginia, teachers used new apps for a year before purchasing the software. Similarly, educators in Cherokee County, Georgia, piloted "five types of math software [and] examined findings about the software from other districts" before making purchasing decisions (p. S10). Piloting before purchasing can save districts millions of dollars.

4. Consider total cost of ownership (TCO) and return on investment (ROI). Doug Johnson, the director of technology for Minnesota's Burnsville-Eagan-Savage Public Schools, strongly recommends that schools calculate the TCO of resources before purchasing them, including the costs of initial hardware, user licenses, technical support, periodic upgrades, and device replacement (Johnson, 2015). Additionally, to maximize ROI, districts and schools should, when possible, purchase resources that can be used in more than one or two disciplines.

5. Conduct needs assessments. Needs assessments help districts to prioritize resources to determine where to allocate funds most effectively. Too often, districts are unclear about their technology needs or even how to evaluate the quality of tech products (Martin & Pines, 2015). Educators should ask the following questions during the needs assessment process (after each question ask, Can we do better?):

• What is the district doing to effectively involve end users (teachers and students) in the procurement process?

• What are the strengths and weaknesses of the district's curriculum and technology review cycles? Do they need to be revised?

• What instructional resources can help faculty better fulfill our school mission and vision?

• What are teachers doing well with students that needs to be supported more vigorously through the procurement process?

• What weaknesses need to be addressed through resource allocation to improve teaching and learning?

• How can district and school personnel ensure that procurement and resource allocation meet the needs of *every* student?

• What are district and school personnel doing to ensure that historically underserved groups (e.g., students with disabilities, English language learners) receive appropriate resources, both human and otherwise?

• What resources can the district procure to help students direct their own learning through technology?

• How are district curriculum, instructional, assessment, and technology resources readying students for an uncertain future?

6. Initiate a resource audit (Grubb, 2009/2010). Evaluate the quality and value of the district's major instructional resources based on their cost, how they align to goals, and the degree to which they help students. It's a good idea to focus on resources that have been used for at least two or three years. Grubb also suggests conducting a waste audit "to see where funds are being misspent" (p. 54). Both resource and waste audits can be conducted as part of a district needs assessment.

7. Promote teacher professional development. Before procuring any major resources, administrators must consider how they are going to help educators learn to use them. Reforms often fail if teacher professional development programs, and books related to the initiatives, are not in the plan.

8. Keep your eyes on the prize. Sometimes a secondary goal will distract us from what ought to be our primary focus. For example, if we buy laptops because they have the screen size required by a testing company but don't consider the end user's experience, then our eyes are off the prize. Classroom teachers need to be actively involved in determining which devices to buy based on student needs.

9. Be a skeptical and discriminating consumer. Vet, vet, and vet again. There are great educational products available, but until a resource has been used effectively in the classroom, success is not guaranteed. It is easy to be swept away by flashy optics during a vendor demonstration, so be wary. If you are thinking of purchasing from a technology start-up, bear in mind that if the company doesn't last, you may encounter service issues.

Being a discriminating consumer also means looking for a great deal. Open education resources (OERs) are online materials—courses, syllabi, lessons, and so on—freely available to all. Popular OER sources such as Khan Academy and Moodle offer blended learning opportunities that millions of learners use every day. Of course, it's still important to be wary of overpromises even if the product is free. Herold (2014a) warns educators about OER companies that claim to be CCSS-aligned but may not be fostering higher-level thinking skills. He also raises concerns about "data-mining techniques and algorithm-based software used to collect information on students and build profiles" (p. 15).

10. Develop relationships with vendors and service providers. Everyone benefits from familiarity and trust building. If relationships are going to last, vendors need to convince districts that they want to help supply them with the most effective products. And when vendors are familiar with a district, they have a better understanding of contextual needs.

11. If the resource is right for students, make a sustained commitment. Investing heavily in resources is futile if educators don't make a long-term commitment to using them. Almost every school practitioner has seen supply rooms filled with stacks of resources that were once popular but are now just accumulating dust. Before making a major investment, ask:

• Does the resource align with our school mission, or is it a fad that may have little to do with teaching and learning?

• If the resource is right for our students, is long-term support in place?

• Do we have the funds required to benefit from the resource for at least the next few years?

• Are we offering teachers sufficient professional development for when the resource becomes part of the fabric of the school?

• What efforts have we made to involve parents and the community in procurement and implementation?

Guidelines for Thoughtful Decision Making

Design thinking, with its focus on accurately identifying the origins of challenges and solving the challenges systemically, provides a framework for decision-making guidelines to help with procurement, needs assessments, and other major school responsibilities (Morena, Luria, & Mojkowski, 2013; Turnali, 2015). The process helps to clarify thinking and focus on priorities. Begin by asking two important questions: (1) Working from the inside out, what do teachers and students perceive to be the major issues that need to be tackled to improve teaching and learning? (2) To address these issues, are educators willing to take risks, make mistakes, and leave their comfort zones? Although decision-making models based on design thinking need not be linear, I've numbered these guidelines for the benefit of readers working in collaborative groups:

1. Take the time to observe, understand, and empathize with the people and issues in schools and classrooms. What are the needs of the students and teachers (the end users)? What are the teachers and students passionate about?

2. Define problems related to improving student performance and teacher success, including root causes, and prioritize them.

3. Brainstorm solutions. Share ideas. Consider pros and cons, a broad range of solutions, and possible unintended consequences.

4. Pilot solutions with end users. Suspend judgment and criticism while experimenting to maximize possibilities.

5. When settling on a solution, work with the end user to refine it.

6. Implement the solution while always observing and respecting classroom challenges.

7. Evaluate the solution and the process that led to it, remembering that success depends on meeting the needs of students and teachers through continuous improvement.

Challenges of Technology Procurement

Technology purchases are particularly consequential because they are so expensive, reducing the cash available for other resources. Herold (2014c) offers three excellent recommendations for educators based on the Los Angeles Unified School District's (LAUSD's) disastrous experience with the Common Core Technology Project. Goals of this initiative included ensuring equity in the distribution of digital tablets, gaining easy access to the CCSS through digital content on the tablets, and preparing students for CCSS assessments. In 2013, the district entered into contracts with Apple and

Pearson to purchase iPads preloaded with Pearson's CCSS-aligned digital curriculum—one for every teacher and administrator and for all 650,000 students in the district. However, in 2014, the superintendent suspended the project on suspicion of "possible manipulation of the bidding process in ways that may have improperly advantaged preferred vendors" (Herold, 2014c, p. 13), student hacking of iPads, and incomplete curriculum resources. Eventually, the entire project was scrapped.

Here are the lessons that Herold (2014c) offers from the LAUSD's experience:

1. **"Urgency is no excuse for poor planning."** According to Herold, Leslie Wilson of the nonprofit One-to-One Institute maintained that the LAUSD used a "spray and pray" approach and was more concerned with getting iPads into student hands than with figuring out the benefits of doing so. She criticized the district for investing millions for digital curriculum resources that, when purchased, included only sample lessons for each grade. What's more, a few days after the iPads were distributed, hundreds of high school students figured out how to gain access to the internet by "disabl[ing] the district's device-management system [and] content-filtering software" (p. 13). Not surprisingly, the school board's report on the project concluded that devices were rushed into use.

2. **"Be wary of one-size-fits-all solutions."** The school board's report took issue with the fact that the project procured only tablets and not laptops, which could possibly have been a better fit for high school students. Consultants assessing the project were also critical of "purchasing a single digital curriculum for all grades from a lone publisher" when so many different content options were available to meet the varied needs of such a large district (p. 13).

3. **"Don't play favorites with vendors."** The report suggested that favoritism might have played a part in the bidding process (though the superintendent rejected the charge). Leslie Wilson reminds educators that the "slickest devices" are captivating, but we must always make "decisions based on the needs of children" (p. 13).

✅ Action Checklist to Avoid Overpromising and Overloading and Effectively Procure Human, Fiscal, and Material Resources

When considering reform initiatives during collaboration:

_____ 1. Resolve that all initiatives and related procurement decisions will align with the school mission statement and student needs.

_____ 2. Conduct an internal audit to determine the number of active reforms in the school or district. Consider the implications of the audit.

_____ 3. Consider the human, fiscal, and material implications of new reforms for current practice.

_____ 4. Refine institutionalized budgetary procedures to fund proposed initiatives by systemically aligning decisions and resources with, at a minimum, curriculum, instruction, assessment, professional development, and capital expenditures.

_____ 5. Allocate time to collaboratively discuss the marketing strategies and procurement guidelines discussed in this chapter.

_____ 6. Be skeptical of quick fixes.

_____ 7. Ensure that any technology plan considers total cost of ownership, return on investment, and infrastructure challenges.

_____ 8. Advocate for students in poverty and underserved students when making decisions about technological resources.

_____ 9. Establish quantitative and qualitative procedures to evaluate reforms under reasonable timelines.

_____ 10. Consider the long-term commitment of faculty and administration to any proposed new initiatives.

Chapter Reflections: Questions and Activities

Please feel free to adapt these questions and activities to meet individual or interactive group goals.

Questions

1. What are the reasons that administrators, teachers, and parents are susceptible to overpromising? To overloading?

2. Review the marketing strategies on pages 59–61. Which ones do you think are most effective? Why? What other strategies should be added to the list?

3. If an initiative's success in another district is cited as part of the pitch to sell your district a program, what questions should you ask?

4. If you were guaranteed funds to sustain three reform initiatives over five years, which ones would you choose? Compare your responses with those of two or three colleagues. Venture a guess: Will your choices align with those of teachers? Administrators? Parents? Students?

5. Review the procurement guidelines on pages 69–73. Select your top two guidelines. Share your ideas with a colleague and indicate why the guidelines resonated with you. What two or three guidelines should be added to the list?

6. Consider the following statement: *Sustained professional development is often overlooked as essential to reform implementation.* Do you agree? Share your thoughts with colleagues. If you believe that professional development is flourishing in your school or district, share why you think so.

7. Based on reading this chapter, what new insights, ahas, or concerns do you have?

8. What beliefs has this chapter reaffirmed?

9. What additional questions need to be asked?

Interactive Activities

Activity: Making Sense of Educational Reforms, Movements, and Trends

1. Every educational era includes a particular set of high-profile reforms, movements, and practices (see Appendix C for a list). Take two to three minutes to write down five to seven important ones from the past decade or two.

2. In groups of two to four, share your lists and discuss. Which of the items listed has had the greatest effect on student learning? Did any of them have a negative effect? Was overpromising an issue?

3. Discuss any takeaways.

Activity: The Astute Consumer

1. For this activity, select two to four educational ads from journals, newspapers, or websites related to instructional resources, technological resources, teaching practices, staff development, and so on.

2. Briefly review the marketing strategies discussed in this chapter.

3. In groups of two to four, examine and discuss the advertisements. What marketing strategies do they use? Which ones are overpromising? How? Which ones are believable? Why?

4. Discuss any takeaways.

Minimizing the Enormous Difficulty of Implementation and Respecting the Change Process

The next project always looks more attractive
. . . it is all promise, fresh, and untried.

Rosebeth Moss Kanter

Two of the most complex human acts are teaching and learning. Educators know that even the most effective lessons have messy classroom moments because teachers are making split-second decisions to promote student success. Thus, implementing classroom practices, even those with a long history of success, can be a hit-or-miss proposition. As Tyack and Cuban (1995) note, "Change where it counts the most—in the daily interactions of teachers and students—is the hardest to achieve and the most important" (p. 10). In this chapter, we will explore the red flag of implementation challenges that traditional reformers all too often don't plan for, as well as guidelines and strategies for surmounting those challenges by learning to respect the change process.

Minimizing the Enormous Difficulty of Implementation

Principle #6: Successful implementation depends on wise insights and directions from the bottom, then support from the top.

"Implementation is everything"—or so William McCallum concluded after observing the unexpected challenges faced by educators trying to implement the Common Core math standards (a document he helped cowrite; Hess & McShane, 2014, p. 1). Reformers commonly err in thinking that implementation will go smoothly simply because they've received initial support for the initiative. Consider: the National Governors Association rolled out the CCSS in 2010 *with bipartisan support*—governors across the political spectrum strongly advocated for the standards. Just a few years later, many of those same governors couldn't run away fast enough from what they now viewed as the federal bureaucracy infringing on local sovereignty.

It is important to distinguish between overpromising (see Chapter 3) and minimizing the challenges of implementation because both red flags foster the harmful notion that change is easy. Overpromising, however, is about manipulating *content* (in the form of language)—"Our teacher evaluation system is guaranteed to improve the skills of every teacher!"—whereas minimizing the challenges of implementation is about denying the importance of *process*, a key aspect of change. In 1987, ASCD published the acclaimed book *Taking Charge of Change*, which offered the following wise words that would soon become a fundamental principle of the literature on change:

> *Change is a process, not an event.* One of the most persistent tendencies of those who do not appreciate the complexities of change is to equate change with handing over a new program, which is an event. This, in fact, was the false tenet on which school improvement was based in the past. We now know that change is a process occurring over time, usually a period of several years. Recognition of this is an essential prerequisite of successful implementation

of change. (italics in original; Hord, Rutherford, Huling-Austin, & Hall, 1987, pp. 5–6)

Experienced change agents understand that change is necessarily nonlinear, without definitive stages or steps. It's messy. Still, a RAND study on school change describes three overlapping phases of the process: "mobilization, implementation, and institutionalization" (Berman & McLaughlin, 1978, p. 13). Darling-Hammond (2010) adds that the success of school change depends on the capacity of educators to learn from experiences and mistakes—which takes time and trust. The long-term commitment of capable faculty and administration is essential. Finally, although implementing change is difficult, that challenge should never derail exchanging innovative ideas to help students.

The Rippling (and Risky) Effects of Implementation

Discussing the CCSS, Hess and McShane (2014) stress that even if educators and the public are comfortable with standards, "the net impact may be negative if implementation is fumbled or undermines other improvement efforts" (p. 207). The CCSS cannot be disengaged from statewide and consortium assessments, technology upgrade decisions, published digital curriculum content, teacher evaluation frameworks, and professional development programs. Adding to the complexity is the fact that student success on state tests depends to some extent on whether the tests are on paper or online: Results from the 2014–2015 Partnership for Assessment of Readiness for College and Careers (PARCC) assessment indicated that students who took tests on paper scored higher than those who did so online (Herold, 2016). These results raise concerns about the validity of test results; some students may not have had the access to technology necessary to become as adept as their peers.

In 2014, politicians, parent groups, and educators in Tennessee decided to reevaluate the state's commitment to the CCSS, starting with disengaging from the PARCC testing consortium. In 2015, the Tennessee legislature voted overwhelmingly to review and replace the CCSS. Of course, this was disconcerting for state educators who had spent years studying and implementing the new standards after receiving a $500 million grant based on the state's commitment to Common Core standards. For three years, 70,000 teachers in the state were involved in professional development related to the CCSS, which included the nation's largest "common-core coaching effort" (Camera, 2014, p. 16). Though the legislation required the state's education board to come up with new English and math standards by the 2017–2018 school year, educators, students, and parents were left with a slew of unanswered questions related to testing, standards, professional development, and student expectations.

The movement to opt out of testing can also be seen as a repudiation of the CCSS. Many parents see no distinction between the standards and end-of-year tests. This kind of grassroots skepticism toward perceived federal encroachment on education led the ESSA to prohibit the U.S. secretary of education from having jurisdiction over a state's academic standards. Former secretary of education Arne Duncan put it plainly: "At the federal, state, and local level, we have all supported policies that have contributed to the problem of implementation" (in Zernike, 2015). Interestingly, and perhaps having learned a lesson from the CSSS implementation, the drafters of the Next Generation Science Standards (NGSS) introduced in 2013 advised educators to concentrate on the standards but hold back on state testing. As the cochair of the National Research Council, James Pellegrino, warned at the time, "Our greatest danger may be a rush to turn the NGSS into sets of assessment tasks for use on high stakes state accountability tests" (Robelen, 2013, p. 13).

In a review of five school improvement efforts, Bryk (2015) skillfully identifies several areas where the reforms fell short of expectations—*all related to implementation difficulties*:

• **Restructuring to create smaller high schools:** "Little guidance existed . . . as to exactly how to transform large, dysfunctional, comprehensive high schools into effective small schools."

• **Employing instructional coaches in schools:** "What coaches actually needed to know . . . and do, and the requisite organizational conditions . . . to carry out the work were left largely unspecified."

- **Supporting principals as instructional leaders:** "Demands on principals' time were already excessive and few or no modifications were offered to relieve those demands."

- **Implementing high-stakes accountability tests:** "Unintended consequences abounded. The incidences of test score cheating accelerated, and select students were ignored."

- **Instituting value-added teacher assessment:** The process "began well before the statistical properties and limits of these methods were appropriately understood." (p. 468)

Organizational Complexity and Outside Forces

Aristotle's famous axiom "The whole is greater than the sum of its parts" is a powerful statement about synergy, but how true it really is depends on how well the parts work together. Senge's (1992) notion of systems thinking, a key to successful organizations, emphasizes the coordination of interrelated parts. Cuban (2013) notes that schools have "hundreds of moving parts," each dependent on autonomous experts, and argues that decision making is compromised because there is no "mission control that runs all these different parts within ever-changing political, economic, and societal surroundings" (p. 156). He contrasts *complex* organizations such as schools with *complicated* rational systems (e.g., NASA) that also have many parts but are steadied by a mission control system that monitors and coordinates workflow with precision. (Of course, even highly disciplined complicated organizations can experience catastrophic breakdowns, as we saw with the *Challenger* and *Columbia* tragedies.)

McChrystal (2015) notes that one characteristic of complex organizations is *unpredictability* due to the sheer number of interactions between component parts. Both unpredictability and unintended consequences are common to change efforts. For example, one unintended consequence of implementing accountability reforms to close achievement gaps has been a narrowing of curriculum, with teachers leaving out content they suspect will be omitted on tests. Another is that teachers may feel less confident about experimenting with new teaching strategies when the curriculum is tightly aligned to state assessments and teacher evaluation.

Outside forces can have an enormous effect on schools (as in the Tennessee example, where fundamental educational issues intersected with the governor's agenda). Danielson (2012) describes another example, when state legislators in Michigan passed laws related to teacher evaluation during the summer—leaving educators with only two months until implementation. "Many . . . [legislators] don't understand the complexity of it," she laments. "I mean, they're not doing it because they're bad people. They just don't know. They don't have a clue what's really involved."

When Egos Get in the Way

Payne (2008) shows the effects of egos on implementation through the reflections of James Lytle, then the superintendent of Trenton Public Schools in New Jersey. Lytle's experiences with several "model developers" engaged in costly long-term reform projects convinced him that developers prefer to stick to their pure models and ignore the need to adapt their plans to local contexts. He noted that "several developers we work with seem slow to learn from the experience of implementation" (p. 163). Lytle also expressed disappointment with the indifference displayed by developers toward recommendations from educators and their failure to appreciate just how much teachers know about school change.

Tyack and Cuban (1995) share a wonderful historical illustration of the tension between impatient technology vendors and their more deliberate school partners. In 1945, about 5 percent of students heard radio broadcasts in schools. Principals in Ohio were surveyed about factors that inhibited radio use. They cited faulty equipment, poor reception, a shortage of school radios, and poor coordination between radio shows and the school curriculum. However, proponents of education by radio faulted *teachers* and their "indifference and lethargy, even antagonism, toward this revolutionary means of communication" for any lack of success (p. 123).

That was 1945. What are the lessons for today?

Complexity and Scaling Up

The success of a program is far from guaranteed when it is transferred from one setting to another. Though we *should* continue to try and scale programs up, we need to be cautious. Payne (2008) offers a strategic approach to scaling up based on the characteristics of successful urban school programs that he refers to as "The Big Six":

Characteristics of High-Impact Urban Instructional Programs

1. Instructional time protected or extended
2. Intellectually ambitious instruction
3. Professional community (teachers collaborate, have a collective sense of responsibility)
4. Academic press combined with social support
5. Program coherence (i.e., instructional focus; are we all on the same page?)
6. Teacher "quality"/diagnostic ability (p. 94)

Payne argues that practitioners in different settings don't always have the necessary knowledge and skills to implement these six proven practices successfully. The solution, he says, is to emphasize different characteristics depending on the situation. Expecting "the whole plan" to be implemented at once is among the reasons reforms so often fail. Payne believes that teacher quality and a teacher's ability to diagnose student problems through feedback are essential. Even in struggling schools, good teachers who monitor student work and adjust their teaching in response can make a big difference. Payne also underscores findings related to academic press and social support since high expectations and challenging students in caring classrooms are critical factors in struggling urban schools.

The Importance of Patience and Time

As a college professor, I had the honor of working with a very successful master's student who was also an outstanding 6th grade teacher. At the time, he was using the groundbreaking National Council of Teachers of Mathematics (NCTM) standards (introduced in 1989, the forerunner to the CCSS) to help his students incorporate critical-thinking skills during math. His master's thesis included astute verbal exchanges among students describing the various ways they were problem solving. I learned a lot talking with this gifted educator about how to unpack student thinking and nurture a classroom where students are comfortable sharing experiences.

Despite his successes, this teacher was often frustrated. "I am a good teacher," he told me once, "but I need more than a few months to successfully understand and implement the NCTM standards. The district is already taking on several new initiatives. I'm just not sure how committed district folks are to the math program."

Tyack and Cuban (1995) note that reformers too often work according to time frames that have little connection to the reality teachers face. Reformers, they note, are "driven by election deadlines, career opportunities, the timing of foundation grants, the shifting attention of the public, or the desire of media people for the dramatic photo opportunity or sound bite" (p. 55). Teachers and students are often caught in the middle.

Based partly on her experiences in Michigan, Danielson (2012) recommends holding off on the evaluation component of any new initiative until teachers understand the framework and are comfortable with it. Her views line up with those of reformers Payne spoke to about their greatest regrets. One theme stood out in their answers: "Take more time . . . for professional development, time for key relationships to develop, time to change teacher beliefs, time for midcourse assessment" (2008, p. 172). Teachers need time to experiment with new ideas; to talk about their practices with colleagues, students, and administrators; and, most of all, to see reforms actually work in the classroom.

Cautionary Examples of Implementation Gone Awry

Jochim (2014) reminds us: "Just because you have buy-in today doesn't mean you'll have it tomorrow" (p. 201). This is all too evident in the examples cited earlier of how quickly resistance to implementing the CCSS grew. Here we'll examine a few examples of implementation gone awry. Consider: What lessons can we learn from these examples to improve our own implementation processes?

The "almost" national history standards of the 1990s. In 1992, the U.S. Department of Education and the National Endowment for the Humanities (NEH) awarded UCLA a grant of $1.6 million to establish a National Center for History in Schools, largely for the purpose of drafting national history standards for grades 5–12 (Meyer, 2014; Ravitch, 2010). Two and a half years later, after the writing of 6,000 drafts by 200 scholars, the primary authors of the standards "met for the last time in a hotel ballroom in Crystal City, Virginia, to celebrate what [they] believed to be a job well done" (Meyer, 2014, p. 125).

It was a done deal—until it wasn't. The diligent effort fell apart just two weeks before the standards were to be unveiled. In October 1994, NEH chair Lynne Cheney, who had initially supported the standards, wrote a scathing attack on the initiative in the *Wall Street Journal* titled "The End of History." The article fueled a national debate on what specific history content should be emphasized in schools. Here's how Cheney's opinion piece began: "Imagine an outline for the teaching of American History in which George Washington makes only a fleeting appearance and is never described as our first president" (1994). Cheney argued that the standards exhibited left-wing bias, noting that McCarthyism was mentioned 19 times, the Ku Klux Klan 17 times, and Harriet Tubman 6 times, while President Ulysses S. Grant was mentioned only once and mentions of Paul Revere, Thomas Edison, the Wright brothers, and Jonas Salk were omitted entirely (Ravitch, 2010).

The scholars behind the standards did not anticipate that their approach to social history, which emphasized race, gender, and class, would create such fallout. In 1995, the Senate disowned the standards in a resounding 99 to 1 vote. In the end, the firestorm left both the Left and Right dissatisfied—and the United States without any national history standards. States were encouraged to create their own standards instead.

Consider what factors were most to blame for this failure of implementation. Were the reformers who drafted the standards overconfident? Did interest groups derail an initiative that they believed dismissed their views? Could a little of both have been the case?

The troubled implementation of the i3 initiatives. The 2009 federal financial stimulus package included an initial $650 million investment to support innovative education programs known as the

Investing in Innovation Fund (i3). By 2016, the initiative had funded 157 projects to the tune of $1.3 billion. Though they were generally well received, Sparks (2016a) notes two i3 projects that achieved only modest results due to implementation difficulties.

In Forsyth, Georgia, schools received a $4.74 million i3 grant to implement the EngageME P.L.E.A.S.E. data management and digital content system. According to Sparks, implementation suffered because the scope of the district's plan was too ambitious, including multiple steps for tracking student progress, aligning students with appropriate programs based on learning styles and interest, and offering flipped classroom alternatives. Because of the program's complexity, three changes in vendors occurred within a few months, and it was midyear before the system was ready to be rolled out. Forsyth's project director, Jason Naile, was pleased with the overall district effort but maintains that more federal guidance early on to assist with the unexpected glitches (such as issues with vendor expertise) would have made early corrections easier to navigate.

Sparks also described difficulties encountered by California's Corona-Norco Unified School District, which was awarded a $5 million i3 grant to implement a hybrid digital program called WriteUp!, which provides students with writing support and feedback aligned with state tests. The program was working well until three years into its implementation, when the state of California decided to switch to a new type of state assessment. As a result, the district could now only use the baseline student assessment data created for evaluating the i3 program. Educators were frustrated because they had seen student writing improve in schools using the program. "The soft data we had was amazing," reported Charla Capps, the director of the program in Corona-Norco. "The improvement teachers were seeing in writing was amazing—but it was all anecdotal" (in Sparks, 2016a). (Though educators were disappointed to lose access to hard data proving the program's worth, thankfully the anecdotal results were enough for educators to continue supporting and expanding it.)

The Chapter Reference Guide (Figure 4) links the red flag of minimizing the enormous difficulty of implementation with the guidelines on respecting the change process by highlighting key chapter points.

FIGURE 4

Chapter Reference Guide: Minimizing the Enormous Difficulty of Implementation and Respecting the Change Process

	Red Flag: Minimizing the Enormous Difficulty of Implementation	Guideline: Respecting the Change Process
Definition	Innocently neglecting or arrogantly discounting the complexity and difficulty of implementing substantive school change initiatives	Valuing process, patience, context, and substance; recognizing that change is meaningful when it most affects teaching and learning
Big Ideas	• Initial enthusiasm for a reform idea should not distract from the amount of work and time required for implementation. • When implementation goes awry, the consequences are often much greater than they initially appear.	• Sustaining the change process is not just about initiating a new or timeless reform; equally important is enhancing trust, risk-taking, collaborative work, and teachers' capacities to grow. • Meaningful change is about student growth and meaningful teacher-student interactions.
Essential Questions	• Why do educators often dismiss the enormous difficulty of implementation? • How can educators prepare for unintended consequences?	• How is school change a moral enterprise? • What needs to occur to keep multiple stakeholders engaged in the long change process?
Drawbacks and Advantages	**Drawbacks:** • Arrogance from reformers who fail to grasp the local context often triggers opposition among teachers and the community. • Disregarding the amount of time and patience needed to learn a new instructional practice is fatal to implementation.	**Advantages:** • When the change process begins with respect for teacher knowledge and professionalism, it can be long-lasting. • Process elements, such as piloting initiatives and addressing context, build credibility for change among stakeholders.
Examples	• Overconfidence regarding implementation of the 1990s history standards • Federal and state legislative initiatives that ignore or undermine previously legislated practices	• Piloting one-to-one technology initiatives before committing major district resources • The Building Assets, Reducing Risks guidance program

Respecting the Change Process

Principle #7: Change that matters takes place in classrooms.

Why do we keep making the same mistaken assumptions about educational change? Educators and the public are particularly susceptible to structural school changes because they can visually be seen. But structural changes have very little effect on student-teacher interactions and classroom instructional content (Cuban, 2013; Elmore, 1995, 1996; Frontier & Rickabaugh, 2014; Tyack & Cuban, 1995). The most successful reforms are those that have been piloted and address pressing local needs. As Schmoker (2014) notes of the CCSS, "The actual list of standards and practices *were never piloted—ever, by anyone*" (italics added; p. 28). (It is fair to ask how this is possible.) Ravitch (2013) agrees about the importance of piloting reforms: "We should try them first on a small scale and gather evidence before applying and mandating new ideas nationwide" (p. 5). Although rarely noted, pilot programs can lead educators to courageously terminate initiatives that show little promise (Levitt & Dubner, 2014).

We often forget that reforms of substance do not need to be revolutionary. Revisiting or refining a classic teaching strategy (e.g., the Socratic method) might just be the key to elevating teacher effectiveness. Additionally, educators need to seek out legitimate research about any reforms under consideration. If implementing initiatives related to student feedback and self-directed learning, for example, John Hattie's (2009) research on student achievement and effect size should certainly be studied.

Morality and Change

The work of educators is a calling—a moral enterprise. Yet, when we are immersed in logistical issues and paperwork related to implementation, this can be easy to forget. The morality of education is reflected in various ways. For one, administrators and teacher leaders have a moral obligation to filter through proposed changes to minimize the adoption of fads and promote reforms of substance. Whether change is the result of mandates, crises, or proactive plans (Benson, 2015), overloading will result if implementation is not adequately monitored. Fortunately, even small gestures can have a big effect. It helps, for instance, for administrators to focus on one or two areas of implementation while everyone gets up to speed with other elements of the process. (Teachers particularly appreciate it when meetings are canceled because "a lot is going on.")

Morality also requires education leaders to make a long-term commitment to reforms. Though the success of any initiative should not depend on a handful of key leaders, it's certainly true that one or two educators can influence a host of variables, such as meeting times, agenda items, space allocation, budgeting, professional development options, and hiring decisions.

Honoring Change: Focus on School Culture and Teaching Practices

Cuban (2011) does not reject "big-ticket" structural changes but suggests that less glamorous reforms make a difference as well, "working directly on individual and collective teacher norms, knowledge, and skills at the classroom level" (p. 30). It is his view that reformers would be much wiser to "focus first on changing norms, knowledge, and skills at the individual and organizational level *before* the focus on changing structure" (italics in original; p. 26). Elmore (1995) likewise notes that when teachers work on their skills, and exchange ideas about what good teaching looks like, they are establishing collaborative norms. Of course, some structural changes are necessary, particularly when the aim is to provide equal access to education (as with desegregation, the Individuals with Disabilities Education Improvement Act, Title IX, English language learner legislation, and state legislation to protect LGBTQ students). As time goes on, it's also vital to build new schools and make technology upgrades.

I believe there are five factors that help to explain the popularity of structural changes:

1. Financial gain. A lot of money is made when structural changes are implemented, with billions of dollars spent on tests, textbooks, curriculum resources, technology, consultants, construction, and instructional programs.

2. Visual impressions. New or updated buildings are prominent examples of "successes" the community can see. Other visual changes might include adopting school uniforms or redesigning the school website.

3. Ease of implementation. Some structural changes are simply *easier* to implement than are new teaching and learning programs. It is easier to write policies, prepare standards, and create strategic plans than it is to actually implement them in schools.

4. Political power. Supporting state receivership of a district and returning a district to local control are both examples of politically motivated structural changes that garner media attention but have little to do with classrooms.

5. Hope. This may be the primary reason behind most structural changes. Regardless of how much evidence exists that structural reforms will have little effect on the classroom, it is simply human nature to keep on trying.

Creating a Culture for Change Built on Trust

When I studied to be a school principal, I learned about the work of Douglas McGregor (1960), the MIT professor who introduced the management world to Theory Y and Theory X. No theory or management strategy helped me more than McGregor's work; I literally staked my career on strategies represented by Theory Y. My coauthor Pam Robbins and I summarized McGregor's ideas in our book *If I Only Knew. . . : Success Strategies for Navigating the Principalship* (1998):

> Theory Y suggests that humans can be trusted and self-directed when committed to an idea. When a leader believes that workers can be trusted, the workers will be more creative and self-directed. . . .

Principals set the tone for this autonomy in how they relate to faculty and staff and in how much support they are willing to provide teachers and counselors in their work with students. (p. 147)

In contrast, "Theory X suggests that if we assume that humans dislike work and cannot be trusted, then we have to coerce them and threaten punishment to get results. With Theory X, humans are by nature irresponsible and must be directed to get work accomplished" (Alvy & Robbins, 1998, p. 147).

Fullan's Four Right Drivers

Theories X and Y relate directly to the change process. As Fullan (2011) notes, "All of the successful school systems have come to trust and respect teachers" (p. 16). Echoing McGregor's Theory Y, Fullan believes that to reduce teachers' distrust, leaders must trust them *before they have earned it*. And yet, the carrot and stick of Theory X remains quite popular among many reformers (e.g., in the form of linking teacher evaluation to student test scores). Fullan insists that when reformers begin with and focus on accountability, standards, and summative assessments as school change drivers, they lose the leverage to affect what takes place in the classroom. He describes drivers as strategies and policies that foster or obstruct successful reform. Fullan maintains that accountability drivers are distant distractions from the instructional core of teaching and learning. He identifies the following four right drivers as essential to successful change efforts:

1. Capacity building (educators foster continuous professional development and student growth)

2. Group work (educators create social capital by pooling skills and making a difference together, not as solo artists, for a common cause)

3. Instruction (educators retain pedagogy as the core driving force for all decisions)

4. Systemic action (educators work as coherently interconnected professionals)

The importance of Fullan's right drivers is reinforced by a recent study on organizational context and culture by Kraft, Marinell, and Yee (2016). The researchers studied 278 New York City middle schools and reviewed more than 31,000 teacher survey responses from 2008 to 2012 to find out how organizational context affects teacher turnover and student achievement. They concluded that reform efforts that concentrate solely on individual teacher effectiveness (e.g., by using a new teacher evaluation system) while failing to address school climate (e.g., how much the teachers respect the principal) miss an opportunity to affect teacher morale and student growth: "Our analyses suggest that when schools strengthen the organizational context in which teachers work, teachers are more likely to remain in these schools, and student achievement on standardized tests increases at a faster rate" (p. 24). Kraft and colleagues reported that the following four factors positively influenced teacher retention: high academic expectations, effective school leadership dedicated to professional development, teacher collaboration built on strong relationships, and increased school safety.

Fullan's Four Wrong Drivers

Fullan's (2011) research also sheds light on the issues of intimidation and arrogance. He describes four *wrong* drivers that inhibit change efforts (though he stresses that all top-performing countries limit the effects of these):

1. Accountability focus (educators are punished or rewarded based on summative student assessments)

2. Individual quality (administrators emphasize individual teacher successes rather than focusing on collective efficacy)

3. Technology dominance (educators believe that technology is more important than pedagogy)

4. Fragmented approach (educators are overloaded with new initiatives without coherence)

Concerning assessment, Fullan (2011) stresses that it is critical to stimulate reform, but only in small doses. He notes that assessments are most valuable when used as formative feedback tools to enhance teaching and foster students' ownership of their work rather than as punitive measures. Also, the four wrong drivers, in moderation, play an important role. For example, technology is an enormous part of schooling today, when used wisely. But technology should not dictate pedagogical decisions; pedagogy should determine how technology is used.

Ancillary Benefits of the Change Process

Culture building, continuous improvement, and creating group norms are all elements of the school change process that emerge as especially important from the writings of Fullan and Kraft and colleagues. Each of these elements can positively affect a school even if reform implementation doesn't last. For example, James Lytle of the Trenton Public Schools discovered that, despite his frustrations with reform efforts, he remained "strongly committed to working with the national reform models not because they are the answer but because they can help organize the search for answers" (in Payne, 2008, p. 163). The work of trying to implement reform gave the teachers in Trenton an opportunity to network with colleagues throughout the country, helping "them become less parochial and more open to change" (p. 164). Other benefits included focusing on evidence of student performance, adopting leadership roles to improve instruction, and coaching and supporting one another.

The Skeptic's Role: Keeping Everyone Honest

The values and norms of a trusting, productive change environment should also leave room for reform skeptics, who are often the first to raise issues that are bound to emerge sooner or later. Those who have served in leadership positions know that distrust leads to mistakes when workers who foresee obstacles fear repercussions for speaking their mind. Perkins and Reese (2014) note that *all* reforms attract "skeptics alongside enthusiasts, late adopters alongside early adopters" (p. 45). To enhance the success of an initiative, they suggest fostering a culture that has "nimble legs" for innovation, where transparency and constructive criticism are welcome and colleagues can decide whether to get involved or not, allowing for "degrees of participation—all-in, half-in, toe-in-the-water, bystander—for now" (p. 46). There are many examples of occasions in and outside of education when insulation from criticism led to leaders making catastrophic errors. Famously, for example, it's very possible that the Vietnam War would not have lasted nearly as long if President Johnson's secretary of defense, Robert McNamara, hadn't been reluctant (out of loyalty or fear) to share his negative assessments of the conflict's progress with the commander in chief.

Arrogance as a Roadblock to Change

Humility may be the most underrated quality of a change agent. Everyone involved in a new initiative needs to listen, ask for support, and revise their views when circumstances merit. Yet overconfidence and arrogance about the effectiveness of a reform often occurs. Otherwise, how can we account for implementing the CCSS without first piloting the initiative? When changes are arrogantly introduced without any solid research or field testing to back them up, the risk of failure is immense. Consider, for example: Why are value-added models (VAMs) used to rate teacher effectiveness when the effectiveness of the models is suspect? According to the American Statistical Association (2014), VAMs "are generally based on standardized test scores, and do not directly measure potential teacher contributions toward other student outcomes. . . . Effects— positive or negative—attributed to a teacher may actually be *caused by other factors that are not captured in the model*" (italics added; p. 2). Thus, trying to motivate teachers to change their behaviors with flawed, punitive measurement tools does little to build confidence and engender professionalism. Teachers know that the VAMs are limited and question the methods of reformers who confidently subscribe to the model.

Success in Action: Building Assets, Reducing Risks

The Building Assets, Reducing Risks (BARR) program, an i3 initiative, is the brainchild of Angela Jerabek, a 9th grade school counselor from Minnesota. BARR is a story of how to effectively implement a school change initiative. In 1998, Jerabek became troubled after discovering that almost half of the freshmen at her high school were failing at least one required academic course—often the first step to dropping out of school. In response, she decided to initiate a program geared to help middle school students successfully transition to high school.

The BARR program creates cohorts of 30 freshmen students "who take the same core reading, math, and science classes together" and "receive a 30-minute weekly lesson on social-emotional skills" (Sparks, 2016b, p. 12). Each week, teacher teams work with each cohort to review individual student goals as well as any issues they may be having outside of school. At Jerabek's high school, the program initially reduced the course-failure rate among freshmen from 47 percent to 27 percent, and it has now remained at or near 20 percent for the past 15 years.

After the program's success in Minnesota, it was awarded an i3 developmental grant of $5 million in 2010. In 2013, especially due to success with low-performing schools, a further $12 million were approved to extend the program to 45 schools in six different states. The networking and exchanging of ideas about BARR strategies among teachers and the strengthening of personal relations with students in various states have become highlights of the program. According to Nadya Dabby of the U.S. Department of Education, the BARR program "has produced pretty incredible results, not just for [Jerabek's] school and in Minnesota, but in districts in California and Maine" (Sparks, 2016b, p. 12).

To evaluate the 2010 grant, a randomized controlled trial was conducted in 2011–2012 with 555 9th graders in California and Maine, showing that BARR participants gained about a half credit more per year and had higher grade point averages than their peers, as well as having improved reading and math standardized test scores. A second control trial of 1,000 students in the same two states, following up the second grant, showed that 61.5 percent of BARR-participating freshmen "passed all of their fall and spring courses in math, reading, and science, compared with only 46.7 percent of nonparticipating students" (Sparks, 2016b, p. 13). In 2015, one Maine high school that adopted the BARR program found that participating students had fully 50 percent fewer absences than non-participants. The high school's principal noted of the program that it "doesn't feel like the next academic fad—it feels like this is something Noble does, who we are"—demonstrating that it met the contextual needs of the school (p. 13). Finally, in 2016, it was announced that BARR would become "the first program to work its way up through all three of i3 grant tiers . . . [winning] a 5-year $20 million scale-up grant to expand to 50 more schools in California, Tennessee, Maine, Minnesota, and Texas" (Sparks, 2016c).

Success in Action: Miami–Dade's One-to-One Computer Initiative

Another successful program is the one-to-one computer initiative that began in 2014 in Miami-Dade County Public Schools—the fourth-largest school district in the United States. Herman (2015) reports that the district smartly put the brakes on its proposed initiative after hearing about the breakdown of the LAUSD initiative (see pp. 74–75) and hurdles in other states involving broken screens, overheated batteries, wireless coverage issues, and digital content unaligned with district curriculum. "We were about ready to make a device selection," said Miami-Dade superintendent Alberto Carvalho, "and I pushed the pause button. I wanted to observe and study what went wrong [in other districts] and why" (p. 18). To that end, Carvalho initiated a three-month review before moving forward. The review pointed to the need for tablets and curriculum to be rolled out gradually, so in the fall of 2014, only 9th grade students were given tablets to use in school and at home, with curriculum material primarily for history classes. Seventh graders were given devices only for in-school use, focusing on civics classes. Carvalho explained: "We have been launching it in waves, specifically for the availability of digital content" (p. 19). Introducing one subject at a time enabled the district to effectively focus on professional development. Reflecting on the implementation process, Carvalho was proud of the program's success. "We took a huge risk that has turned into a huge reward," he said (p. 19). The greatest satisfaction, he said, came from seeing students with no previous access to technology enjoy their digital devices. Still, Carvalho and the IT Department noted glitches involving password errors, bandwidth issues, and time management challenges to accommodate faculty training.

In her article on the Miami-Dade program, Herman (2015, pp. 18–19) provides the following excellent guidelines for avoiding implementation mistakes:

- **Articulate your vision.** Too often, districts give students devices before figuring out the learning goals, why the devices are being distributed, or what digital curriculum is to be uploaded.
- **Start small.** Pilot the project in one grade at a time—urgency often leads to poor decision making.
- **Get schools tech-ready.** Infrastructure planning is critical before distributing any technological resources necessary for the initiative. It might take a year to wire schools for bandwidth.
- **Prepare teachers.** Ensure that all teachers receive professional development to help them implement the initiative successfully.
- **Engage the community.** Districts need to involve parents in the implementation effort lest they perceive the reforms as simple, routine upgrades.
- **Build a brand.** Effectively marketing the initiative helps to clarify goals for stakeholders.
- **Make content king.** Innovation occurs when a variety of digital sources are captured on tablets beyond traditional textbook content to help students mine and interact with proprietary and open-source resources.

Tasked with reviewing what went wrong with LAUSD's aborted change effort, former associate superintendent Judy Burton concluded,

It's not about the devices. We could have a device in the hand of every student as we speak, but that does not mean that you have succeeded in introducing integrated learning in the classroom. Teachers need a clear instructional strategy for device use to personalize and differentiate learning. (in Herman, 2015, p. 19)

Four Lessons About Change

Teacher leaders and school principals eventually learn the following four lessons about change:

1. Regardless of how revolutionary, innovative, or seemingly fitting an idea appears to be, it will not succeed unless leaders respect the fidelity of the change process. Change occurs on the dual tracks of ideas and process.

2. Reforms are simply ideas on paper until teachers decide otherwise. Regardless of how much top-down praise it receives, an initiative will have little effect until classroom teachers decide to implement it.

3. Change is not just about introducing new, innovative ideas; it also involves affirming, supporting, and, when necessary, reintroducing timeless ideas of substance. For example, the commitment to teach 21st century skills can overshadow what cognitive scientists continually remind us: "Students need to know facts" (Riley, 2016, p. 36).

4. Benefits of the change process extend beyond implementing a new initiative. When the process works, individual and group capacity flourishes through collaboration, risk-taking, and feedback.

☑ Action Checklist to Avoid Minimizing the Enormous Difficulty of Implementation and Promote Respecting the Change Process

When considering reform initiatives during collaboration:

_____ 1. Present evidence that initiatives will positively affect student learning and teacher success in classrooms.

_____ 2. Support strategies that address the value of *ideas* under consideration while also honoring critical aspects of the change *process.*

_____ 3. Ensure that teachers are engaged in the decision-making process regarding new initiatives so that their expertise can be tapped.

_____ 4. Plan and implement professional development activities aligned with reforms.

_____ 5. Commit to achieving essential culture-shaping goals that occur with successful change (e.g., building trust, promoting risk-taking, strengthening social capital).

_____ 6. Collaboratively consider and proactively address possible roadblocks to implementing initiatives.

_____ 7. Assess the local school or district context before approving any initiative that has "succeeded" when scaled up elsewhere. (Of course, if the initiative is government-mandated, you're required to proceed, but fine-tune the initiative to address local needs.)

_____ 8. Consider the holistic implications of initiatives for students, teachers (e.g., professional development), curriculum, instruction, assessment, the school budget, and the community.

_____ 9. Assess whether piloting the proposed initiatives is necessary.

_____ 10. Commit to keeping staff, parents, and the community involved and informed throughout the implementation process.

Chapter Reflections: Questions and Activities

Please feel free to adapt these questions and activities to meet individual or interactive group goals.

Questions

1. Your district or school is considering adopting an initiative that has been successfully implemented in another setting. What contextual issues and questions need to be addressed? (Before answering the question, select a specific initiative.)

2. Consider an initiative that you were positively fired up about but that eventually lost momentum. What were some of the unforeseen roadblocks?

3. Recall the section in this chapter on difficulties implementing the radio as a teaching tool in the 1940s. What parallels can be drawn with today? Are we doing a better job of implementing technology now?

4. Why is it never a guarantee that reforms will be sustained? What variables of the change process can enhance the likelihood that they will be?

5. Select an initiative that you strongly support and try to see it through the eyes of a skeptic. What questions do you want answered? Do you now think the initiative should be abandoned?

6. What would you add to the four lessons about change listed on page 100?

7. Based on reading this chapter, what new insights, ahas, or concerns do you have?

8. What beliefs has this chapter reaffirmed?

9. What additional questions need to be asked?

Interactive Activities

Activity: Gap Analysis

A gap analysis gives organizations an opportunity to compare current with desired conditions. (This activity requires at least four participants, with teams of at least two each.)

1. Each team writes a list of three to five statements describing the characteristics of a school or district culture that would be likely to embrace the change process. Consider such elements as norms, values, beliefs, and assumptions. Then, teams compare and synthesize the best ideas to create a master list of three to five statements.

2. This step can be collaborative or independent, dependent on participants' comfort levels. On a scale of 1 to 7, rate each statement on the master list according to how well it applies to your school or district (1 = not ready for change; 7 = ideally ready). What conclusions can you draw about your school or district's readiness to implement change?

3. Discuss any takeaways.

Activity: The Best-Laid Plans of Mice and Men Often Go Awry

This activity works best with at least two groups of three to five participants. Each group should select one reform initiative that is currently popular.

1. Each group takes about 10 minutes to create a hypothetical school with a specific demographic (e.g., rural, high school, English language learner students, free and reduced lunch, special education, AP students, faculty) and school culture (norms, values, and beliefs). Alternatively, groups can select an existing school.

2. Each group takes 15 to 20 minutes to develop both a worst-case scenario and a best-case scenario for implementing the selected initiative in the chosen school. Consider the RAND Corporation's three overlapping phases of the change process: "mobilization, implementation, and institutionalization" (Berman & McLaughlin, 1978, p. 13).

3. Individual group members take two to three minutes to record personal reflections on the exercise.

4. Groups share out highlights of the exercise. What common challenges were there?

5. Discuss any takeaways.

Eyes Off the Prize and Sustaining a Coherent School Mission and Vision

---

We often use the wrong tests to make our
most important educational decisions.

James Popham

It's easy to get distracted by promising new ideas and attractive resources. Unfortunately, when distractions seize the spotlight, core teaching and learning concerns fade into the shadows—*primary goals* are undermined by *secondary interests,* and a red flag needs to be raised. The phrase "eyes off the prize" refers to this condition, when subsidiary goals diminish, distract, and obstruct the influence of more important goals. One good example of eyes off the prize in education is when teachers narrow their teaching regardless of students' curriculum needs to address topics they believe will be on high-stakes tests. Another example is when districts make ill-advised technology purchases to get ahead of the curve *before* considering whether they are aligned to their missions and technology plans.

There is no simple solution to avoiding distractions—it's difficult to take our eyes off shiny objects! It certainly helps to remain grounded, guided by the school's mission and vision. The *mission* forces us to ask: Why do we, as a school, exist? What is our purpose? The *vision* is how we visualize the mission in action. The mission and vision guidelines, described later in the chapter, will serve as countermeasures to the eyes off the prize red flag. When striving to adhere to the mission, educators must ask:

- What outcomes do we desire for our students?
- How will our students be different as a result of their education?
- What are we doing to maintain program coherence?
- How are we closing the achievement and opportunity gaps among our students?
- Are we sufficiently serving our special education students and English language learners?
- What are we doing to ensure that each instructional resource, program, or service purchase will keep us on track guided by our mission?

Words matter. The mission and vision tie educators to a school's purpose—a strong deterrent for getting distracted by gadgets and programs that have little effect on teaching and learning.

Eyes Off the Prize

> Principle #8: When you fall in love with a reform initiative, move it from the *heart* to the *head*. Then ask, Is this reform a shiny object, or will it affect student learning beyond today?

Goal displacement occurs when well-intended ideas result in unintended consequences. For example, federally mandated high-stakes testing was *intended* to advance achievement in English language arts (ELA) and math for all students; instead, the achievement gap remains, the ELA and math curricula were narrowed, and cheating scandals related to high-stakes tests occurred in several major cities (Ravitch, 2014). Ravitch further notes that when teacher evaluations are linked to student test scores, many teachers, to protect their salaries and careers, feel pressured to ignore the neediest students to help students on the testing "bubble."

ASCD has been an outspoken critic of the misuse of high-stakes tests. In 2015, the organization issued a "Testing and Accountability Statement" calling for a "two-year moratorium on using state assessments for high-stakes purposes" (ASCD, 2015b). The statement did not call for the elimination of state tests but recommended that a multimetric approach be used to assess student growth. Unintended consequences of high-stakes testing noted by ASCD include over-testing, using tests to evaluate teacher performance, narrowing the curriculum, and de-emphasizing the importance of untested subjects. Suggesting that tests have regrettably become a main driver of school improvement at the expense of more effective measures, the ASCD statement calls for a conversation among educators to advance school readiness, teacher performance, and school quality as part of a whole child approach to education.

High-Stakes Testing and Social-Emotional Learning

In 2015, federal legislators, reacting to the criticism of the NCLB accountability and testing approach, included in the ESSA the opportunity to assess at least one nonacademic indicator of student or school success, such as school safety, student engagement, or school climate (ASCD, 2015a). Should issues related to character, such as social-emotional learning, be used to judge the quality of a school? Duckworth (2016) takes a strong stand against this approach, insisting that "we're nowhere near ready—and perhaps never will be—to use feedback on character as a metric for judging the effectiveness of teachers and schools. We shouldn't be rewarding or punishing schools for how students perform on these measures." Not surprisingly, teachers might feel compelled to narrow the curriculum of character strengths they teach to help students do better on social-emotional learning tests. Will high-stakes testing now affect how teachers approach social-emotional learning (e.g., should I drop empathy and perseverance from the curriculum?)?

Working on Standards: Don't Forget the Teacher

Several years ago, I attended a workshop on statewide curriculum standards. The presenters did a fine job of reviewing expectations related to standards, content, and skill development, demonstrating how complexity increased with each grade level. However, I was stunned during the workshop by the presenters' failure to mention the role that teachers play in writing individual lessons and, most importantly, delivering instruction. The word "teacher" was barely mentioned during the workshop. It was as if developing standards were the final act. Fullan (2011) stresses that "focusing on standards and [summative] assessments does not highlight adequately ... instructional improvements" (p. 8). He refers to the daily work of instructional improvement as the "learning-instruction-assessment nexus that is at the heart of driving student achievement" (p. 8). Yet the workshop presenters concentrated solely on a structural change—standards—rather than on the role of teachers and the centrality of instruction and student work to school change.

Technology and Taking Our Eyes Off the Prize

The flipped classroom has been a popular and important educational trend since its introduction in 2007, helping many teachers to personalize instruction. After researching and successfully using the practice for several years, Moran and Young (2015) decided to "advocate for a more thoughtful and complex approach to flipping the classroom to avoid the pitfalls of perpetuating another educational fad" (p. 46). Specifically, Moran and Young suggest that math and science classes may be better suited for flipping than humanities classes, which focus so much on writing, performance, and discussion. These comments are refreshing; Moran and Young, enthusiastic flipped classroom advocates, also recognize that its use is not unlimited. They are concerned that teachers in all disciplines are being pressured to flip their classrooms simply because the strategy is popular. To illustrate, they cite a North Carolina English Teachers' Association conference in which all the teachers in their session felt pressured to use flipped instruction.

Cooperative learning is another popular strategy that has too often been overused at the expense of a contextually more effective approach. For some teachers cooperative learning is the default instructional strategy. Wiggins and McTighe stress that although activity-oriented strategies are important, teachers should decide on unit outcomes and student learning targets *before* choosing instructional strategies and resources (in Varlas, 2015). Choosing from an array of instructional strategies—flipped exercises, lectures, cooperative learning, project-based activities, lab experiments, field trips, modeling, role-playing, guided practice, brainstorming, and so on—should *follow, not precede,* defining unit goals. McTighe notes that if student outcomes and goals are not the first priority, activity-oriented learning strategies can become "the end in itself" because the lessons are fun and engaging (p. 4). As Wiggins reminded us, "It's possible to build a model of a working roller coaster but not learn any physics" (p. 4).

According to Cuban (2013), research doesn't support the perception among many that new technologies have changed teaching practices or improved test scores. In fact, Daccord and Reich (2015) argue that unless teachers receive significant professional development, they are likely to use technology to support present practices. Conversations between technology providers and educators should always begin with teaching and learning concerns, so that recommendations can be made *within an academic context*. As with other instructional tools, there will be times when digital devices should not be used. Can everyone live with that?

Eyes Off the Prize and Testing

Jane David (2011), director of the Bay Area Research Group, notes that "when the stakes are high, it's likely that what's missing from the tests will disappear from the curriculum" (p. 78). During the NCLB era, research revealed that "the content of the tests had effectively become the learning goals" (p. 79). In elementary schools, time allocated in class for the two tested areas, math and reading, increased substantially (by 37 percent and 47 percent, respectively) at the expense of other subjects (e.g., science, social studies, physical education, art) and activities like recess. As the popular education refrain goes, "What gets measured gets treasured." A personal experience reinforced this expression for me (see "A Lesson Learned").

This story highlights how secondary interests can sideline primary goals. Interestingly, in a summary of Au's 2007 synthesis of 49 studies on high-stakes testing and curriculum, David (2011) reports that the testing led to *more* teacher-centered instruction rather than less. Teachers felt the need to control and narrow instructional goals to meet testing expectations. Ravitch (2014) estimates that because of federal mandates, states spent hundreds of millions of dollars and districts spent up to 20 percent of their time on preparing for high-stakes tests. She writes: "Testing, I realized with dismay, had

A LESSON LEARNED

High-Stakes Tests Lead to Less, Rather Than More, Instruction

About a decade ago, I attended a daylong meeting of an educational association board on which I serve. New state standards in reading and math had recently been issued and were distributed at the meeting. During our lunch break, I noticed four or five veteran elementary teachers examining the standards. I was impressed by their level of engagement and saw that they were already enthusiastically using highlighters to target key content, concepts, and skills that they would be teaching.

I walked over to the teachers and told them how impressed I was that they were already highlighting key teaching points. In fact, that wasn't what they were doing at all; rather, they were highlighting standards that were omitted on the last couple of high-stakes state tests. As one of them told me, "We are highlighting this section because it includes content we are *not* going to teach—it's not going to be on the test." These teachers, who knew their students best, were preparing to omit material that may have been right for their students. They felt the pressure of high-stakes testing and knew their schools were being evaluated and compared based on student test scores.

become a central preoccupation in the schools and was not just a measure, but *an end in itself.* . . . [A]ccountability as written into federal law was not raising standards but dumbing down the schools" 2010, pp. 12–13).

Popham (2016) notes that $350 million awarded in 2010 by the U.S. Department of Education to two testing consortia "were supposed to permit state-to-state [and] national comparisons regarding students' mastery of the CCSS curriculum targets" (p. 45), but implementation has been problematic. The data the two testing consortia report are incompatible (based on test items), notes Popham, and many teachers feel that the test score information provided is too broad to use for instructional purposes. *If the testing cannot be used to improve instruction, then why take the tests?*

In 2013, New York State decided to administer its new CCSS-aligned reading and math tests despite the consensus that students were not yet ready to take the exams and teachers were still familiarizing themselves with the standards. The results for 3rd through 8th grade: "Across the state . . . 31 percent of students passed the exams in reading and math, compared with 55 percent passed in reading and 65 percent in math last year" (Hernández & Gebeloff, 2013). In New York City, scores showed 26 percent passing in English compared to 47 percent the previous year and 30 percent passing math compared to 60 percent. In Rochester, only *5 percent* of students passed in math and reading.

The rationale for administering the tests was that students needed to learn how to take more rigorous exams even if they were not yet prepared. New York City mayor Mike Bloomberg called the tests results "very good news" because they showed that the new exams were more rigorous. By contrast, Chrystina Russell, the principal of Global Tech Preparatory in East Harlem, was quite dismayed. Her school, with its large population of students in poverty, saw scores drop from 33 percent in English to 7 percent and from 46 percent in math to 10 percent. Russell's frustration was obvious. "Now we're going to come out and tell everybody that they've accomplished nothing this year and we've been pedaling backward?

It's depressing" (Hernández & Gebeloff, 2013). Reporting almost a year later after the new exams were administered, Hernández (2014) noted that students were still feeling the effects of the previous year's exam. Chrispin Alcindor, a 4th grader at Public School 397 in Brooklyn, put it bluntly: "If I don't pass the test, I will feel miserable and never leave my room."

The opt-out movement in several states, the four-year moratorium on using state tests to evaluate teachers in New York, and the national debate on the CCSS are all at least partially a result of the careless rush to implement tests and standards. By far the most important victims of this rush have been students who've seen their confidence deflated and even their desire to remain in school put at risk. Hopefully these lessons will not go unnoticed by policymakers and legislators when they create laws to improve schools.

The Chapter Reference Guide (Figure 5) links the eyes off the prize red flag with the sustaining a coherent school mission and vision guidelines, highlighting key chapter points.

Sustaining a Coherent School Mission and Vision

> **Principle #9: Publicly affirm and share the school mission because when frustrations capture the day, it is the anchor reminding everyone that education is sacred.**

For several years, I was responsible for facilitating a series of seminars for a school district leadership team. We designed the seminars around topics and initiatives that would strengthen the team's leadership capacity, reinforce current school initiatives, and keep the administrators abreast of educational reforms.

One summer, after reading an inspiring leadership book, I scheduled an appointment with the superintendent to plan the fall seminars. I was enthusiastic about sharing what I had learned and hoped he would agree that the book should be read by administrators and used as a major seminar resource. After I shared my thoughts, the superintendent looked at me, smiled, and said, "Harvey, what does

FIGURE 5

Chapter Reference Guide: Eyes Off the Prize and Sustaining a Coherent School Mission and Vision

	Red Flag: Eyes Off the Prize	Guideline: Sustaining a Coherent School Mission and Vision
Definition	When primary goals are undermined by secondary interests	Making decisions about student needs based upon beliefs about how to provide an exceptional K–12 education to advance their future success
Big Ideas	• High-stakes testing expectations have narrowed the curriculum and hindered the range of teaching practices needed to help students succeed. • The effectiveness of classroom technology tools is undermined when they are purchased and used before sound pedagogical and professional development decisions are made.	• A district or school's mission is a moral imperative, reminding educators, students, and the community that the purpose of schooling is to provide all students with the educational tools to succeed in life. • Mission and vision serve as powerful tools for sustaining what works while avoiding the lure of educational fads.
Essential Questions	• What can educators do when federal and state mandates limit instructional options for students? • Why do quick fixes continue to attract educators, weakening mission coherence?	• How can educators make their district or school mission and vision living documents? • When is it appropriate for a district or school to review or revise its mission and vision?
Drawbacks and Advantages	**Drawbacks:** • High-stakes testing has become an end in itself, reducing opportunities for many students (particularly those already underserved). • The pressure to make short-term gains impedes sound decision making related to long-term teaching and learning goals.	**Advantages:** • A school or district mission serves to support and sustain present reforms that work when impatient stakeholders want to move on to the next big thing. • As a living document, the mission is a template for change when called for.
Examples	• Selecting trendy class activities before considering unit outcomes • High-stakes test screen size requirements dictate technology purchases.	• The Singapore American School mission and strategic goals • Community demographic changes lead to revision of the mission.

this book have to do with our district mission and vision and our current initiatives?"

Oops. He was right—I should have known better. I ignored the mission and vision initiatives for a new idea I fell in love with to get the attention of the leadership team. We then had a very fruitful discussion about coherence and keeping our eyes on the prize.

This experience proved to be a great personal lesson. Although I understood the importance of mission and vision, my enthusiasm for a new idea had distracted me from it. All too often, coherence is lost because of initiatives that ignore mission and vision. Thinking about mission and vision involves *taking a coherent and holistic approach* that weighs the alignment of curriculum, instruction, assessment, and professional development with student equity issues related to achievement differences, opportunity gaps, and special services.

Reassessing the Mission

Although a mission provides the light that guides a school or district, it is hardly as immutable as a lighthouse. Sometimes educators need to reassess the mission for good reason. Perhaps their school or district is struggling with low graduation rates, an insufficient number of advanced classes, underachieving special education students, too many bullying incidents, or a disturbingly high degree of teacher turnover. Under such circumstances, it is appropriate to share data about what is and is not working, examine values and beliefs, and reassess the mission. To quote one of the National Policy Board for Educational Administration's professional standards, educators should "review the school's mission and vision and adjust them to changing expectations and opportunities for the school and changing needs and situations of students" (2015, p. 9).

When reassessing a school's mission, the conversation should begin with the following three fundamental questions: Why do we exist? What is our purpose? What are our core values? In his biography of Steve Jobs, Isaacson (2011) concludes that one of Jobs's great skills was filtering out distractions to concentrate on one or two big product ideas at a time, always aiming for simplicity. As the head of

Apple's design team, Jony Ive, stated, "You have to deeply understand the essence of a product in order to be able to get rid of the parts that are not essential" (p. 343). Jobs and Ive clearly understood why Apple exists and what the company's purpose was, which Isaacson called "fundamental principles"—beliefs that dictated decisions and behaviors at the company.

Success in Action: Mission, Vision, and Strategic Planning

Strategic planning in schools frequently begins with intense conversations about essential beliefs (i.e., "fundamental principles") to clarify the mission and vision and develop strategic objectives. For example, when I served as the high school principal at the Singapore American School, personnel from the various school divisions, along with middle and high school students and community stakeholders, developed seven strategic goals to be accomplished over five years (see "A Lesson Learned" in Ch. 3, p. 68). We also revised the school's mission statement to read as follows:

> The mission of the Singapore American School is to provide each student the highest quality American educational experience that inspires a passion for learning and intellectual vitality; that instills the competence, confidence, and courage to contribute to the global community and to pursue her or his dreams.

The seven strategic goals addressed professional development, acquisition of resources, technology integration, curriculum and instructional changes, assessment tools, fostering an open dialogue with the school and community, and creating partnerships to foster student community service. We took special pride in the mission statement because the phrase "pursue her or his dreams" came directly from students. To this day, I can see the faces of the students who suggested those words.

Three years after adopting the strategic plan, we narrowed the number of goals to pursue because we saw firsthand that we were overloading ourselves with reforms. This kind of modification was key to its continued success.

Success in Action: Mission, Technology, and the Arts

Daccord and Reich (2015) tell us that *successful technology imple-mentation occurs in schools that already have a strong pedagogical mission and vision.* They humorously quote a math teacher's response to an unclear vision of technology to reinforce their point: "If iPads are the answer, what is the question?" (p. 20). When used purpose-fully, technology allows students to express their work in a variety of creative ways integrating academics, technology, and the arts. A strong pedagogical mission enables teachers and students to grow "from using tablets for consumption to using them for curation, creation, and connection" (p. 29). The authors offer examples of purposely implemented technology used to enhance research skills, student collaboration, and argumentation abilities and to showcase products beyond a class audience. One example they share is of a 15-year-old high school student's video for history class:

> The engrossing 12-minute clip features hand-drawn animation, sketch notes, music, and student narration. . . . Motivated by [YouTube] interest, the student asked [the teacher] if she could work on her project some more. She wanted to improve her video and boost viewership. If you now Google "Adam Smith and Karl Marx," you'll find that her video ("Adam Smith vs. Karl Marx: The Industrial Revolution") has more than 80,000 views. (Daccord & Reich, p. 21)

In the examples cited by Daccord and Reich, pedagogy and tech-nology were integrated to advance the mission of self-directed stu-dent learning. The authors emphasize that getting technology into the hands of students and teachers is only a first step; teachers need to be supported as they experiment with the technology to achieve a 21st century vision of learning.

✓ Action Checklist to Avoid Taking Your Eyes Off the Prize and Promote Sustaining a Coherent School Mission and Vision

When considering reform initiatives during collaboration:

_____ 1. Provide evidence that initiatives align with the school or district mission and protect the interests of underserved students.

_____ 2. Examine and collaboratively discuss whether recent reforms (including those mandated by the government) have allowed subsidiary interests to obstruct the pursuit of primary teaching and learning objectives.

_____ 3. Assess whether initiatives currently under consideration will promote primary objectives over subsidiary interests. If not, how is the school or district going to respond?

_____ 4. Assess whether the mission and vision statements need to be revisited (by emphasizing helping underserved populations, for example).

_____ 5. On occasion, consider advancing initiatives that "stray" from the school mission but meet student needs. If the initiatives are successful, consider revisiting the mission.

_____ 6. Support technology reforms that are driven by student needs and pedagogy rather than popularity or other factors unrelated to teaching and learning.

_____ 7. Develop relationships with technology vendors who seek to understand pedagogy, student needs, and local context.

_____ 8. Review the mission and vision periodically to reaffirm to faculty, staff, and the community the importance of modeling democratic values in schools so that each student has an equal chance at success.

Chapter Reflections: Questions and Activities

Please feel free to adapt these questions and activities to meet individual or interactive group goals.

Questions

1. What are two examples of taking your eyes off the prize that you have experienced or observed? Examples may or may not be related to education.

2. How can districts, schools, and individual practitioners counter subsidiary interests obstructing primary goals?

3. Based on your experiences and observations, have schools successfully integrated technology in the classroom? What has worked? What would you change?

4. What are two or three core values that you think should provide the foundation for a personal or organizational mission statement?

5. What was your best school experience ever? Do you recall your worst school experience? How do these experiences affect your teaching or leadership work? Share your thoughts with colleagues.

6. Review your school or district mission and vision. What are their strengths? Is it time to refine or make major changes?

7. Based on reading this chapter, what new insights, ahas, or concerns do you have?

8. What beliefs has this chapter reaffirmed?

9. What additional questions need to be asked?

Interactive Activity: Mini-Strategic Planning Workshop

1. Create groups of two to four. Each group member should spend five minutes alone reflecting on the following question: What is the purpose of an education?

2. Group members share their ideas with one another.

3. Group members home in on the most popular ideas (i.e., what resonated with you?) and reach a group consensus on the purpose of an education.

4. Groups share out their consensus results and together create a joint statement about the purpose of an education. If groups cannot reach a consensus, consider what obstacles were in the way.

5. Discuss any takeaways.

Historical Amnesia and Embracing Timeless and Eclectic Teaching Practices

---

*Those who cannot remember the past
are condemned to repeat it.*

George Santayana

When a new educational reform is introduced, or when a classic one is reintroduced, the chances of success are enhanced if the reform is examined and fine-tuned through the lens of history. Unfortunately, educators too often develop *historical amnesia* and make little or no effort to explore the antecedents of proposed reforms. Viewing initiatives from a historical perspective allows us to address such vital questions as the following:

- What is the lineage of the initiative?
- Has the initiative been tried in a previous era? If yes, how was it received?
- Is the initiative truly as effective as advocates assert, or is it just "old wine in a new bottle"?

If the initiative is being reintroduced, it is essential to also answer the following questions:

- Has new research surfaced warranting a reintroduction of the initiative?
- Was the initiative ahead of its time before? Was it too controversial?
- How can the initiative be refined so that it is more successful this time?

Historical amnesia renders these questions unasked and unanswered. It is a red flag because it denies educators the opportunity to explore the past to inform decisions about present-day reforms. Consider today's popular maker movement, which has a rich history going back to John Dewey's University of Chicago Lab School in the 1890s. Today's maker movement advocates *can improve their practice and avoid past mistakes* by taking a historical journey to review Dewey's "learning by doing" approach, the project method promoted by William Heard Kilpatrick in the 1920s, and the Progressive Education Association's "Eight-Year Study" into inquiry learning in the 1930s and early 1940s.

In Kilpatrick's famous 1918 article on the project method, he predicts that skeptics would perceive the movement as "the latest arrival to knock for admittance at the door of educational terminology." Kilpatrick asserted that complex projects (e.g., building a boat) could be construed as purposeful academic activities. In Dewey's time, some progressive educators were opposed to any structured curriculum or formal instruction at all, believing that it stifled creativity and risk-taking. Today's maker movement advocates can learn invaluable lessons from these historical examples because they will undoubtedly be criticized for engaging in too much child's play and using technology unmoored from curriculum.

Structure was always essential to Dewey's methodology. At his lab school, what looked like pure play to others was actually a set of deliberately scaffolded activities that imparted academic knowledge (e.g., in history, math, Shakespeare, Latin) to students. Ravitch's (2000) description of Dewey's philosophy provides critical advice for all proponents of the maker movement:

[Dewey] insisted that there was no conflict between child and curriculum, between the child's experiences and subject matter. The relationship between the child and the curriculum was a *continuum*, he wrote, not an opposition: "[T]he child and the curriculum are simply two limits which define a single process. Just as two points define a straight line, so the present standpoint of the child *and* the facts and truths of studies define instruction." (italics added; p. 172)

For Dewey, activities are tied to curriculum goals and the unique needs of each child. Unfortunately, educators tend to fall into "either/or" traps, discarding a range of ideas on the continuum Ravitch mentions: Instruction is *either* student-centered *or* subject-centered, curriculum is based *either* on content *or* on 21st century skills, science is taught *either* through books and lectures *or* through labs. It's easy to forget that effective teachers are *eclectic practitioners* who use *both* student- and subject-centered practices. Educators must not get caught up in contrived polarities. "Instead of being oppressed by the 'Tyranny of the OR,'" write Collins and Porras (2002), "highly visionary companies liberate themselves with the 'Genius of the AND'—the ability to embrace both extremes of a number of dimensions at the same time" (p. 44).

It's unfortunate that polarizing ideas have dominated educational history in uncompromising pendulum swings, leading practitioners to think that each era is an about-face from the preceding one. "We just go from one extreme to another," reflects the frustrated teacher. "Today the Common Core standards emphasize expository reading and writing; tomorrow a new reform will reverse the trend and promote more fiction and poetry." Collins and Porras's "Genius of the AND" approach offers a much more promising strategy for educators by encouraging them to build on previous practices. The approach embraces the paradox of pursuing what some might see as polar objectives, seeking to synthesize the best ideas from both. Collins and Porras, in addition to bridging polar ideas, stress the importance of core values, *the timeless ideals that anchor organizations during rocky times,* throughout the process. Timeless and eclectic teaching practices, anchors for educators and an antidote to historical amnesia, will be examined later in the chapter.

Historical Amnesia

Principle #10: Proponents of proposed reforms should enthusiastically share the reform's "ancestry"; failing to do so should immediately raise credibility issues.

One of the most successful and practical educational programs of the past 20 years is Wiggins and McTighe's Understanding by Design, which is built on the core notion of backward design. Wiggins and McTighe applaud and credit the educator who greatly influenced their essential backward design ideas. "This view is hardly radical," they write in their 1998 book introducing the program. "Ralph Tyler . . . described the logic of backward design clearly and succinctly about 50 years ago" (p. 8). They credit Tyler with significantly influencing their curriculum work and highlight his emphasis on "continuity, sequence, and integration" (p. 154). (They also note that Tyler was John Dewey's student—a detail that certainly adds some perspective to their important work.)

Clearly, we should celebrate these historical links between old and new ideas, particularly as this helps us to see what has worked previously as well as today's practices. The historical background of a reform—all the way back to the roots of the idea—can shed much light on its inner workings, much as a solid review of the literature sheds light on a research study.

Unfortunately, some reformers and policymakers believe it is fruitless to explore the history of education or hear practitioners talk about previous experiences. After all, they ask, why should we seek insights from educators who created mediocre or failing schools? These reformers prefer to exchange ideas about education with the corporate, higher education, and foundation worlds (Tyack & Cuban, 1995). All educators should certainly welcome fresh ideas from inside and outside the K–12 education community, lest they fall into a narrative trap. However, when policymakers or innovators from outside of education propose "new ideas" without checking the historical trail, they may be unaware whether the ideas are actually new. The Stanford linguist Arnold Zwicky calls this dilemma the *recency illusion*—the tendency to believe that ideas are new regardless of how long they've been around (Rickford, Wasow, Zwicky, & Buchstaller, 2007).

The Recency Illusion, Relabeling Practices, and Helen Parkhurst

The recency illusion has important implications for education. In 1970, the educational historian Herbert Kliebard, lamenting the failure of school change efforts, concluded that "new [educational] breakthroughs are solemnly proclaimed when in fact they represent minor modifications of earlier proposals" (in Goodman, 1995, p. 2). Today, by failing to review the literature behind proposed initiatives, reformers are likely to repeat past mistakes.

Beginning teachers often have no choice but to employ the latest innovations their districts are promoting, whereas seasoned professionals have the confidence and experience to decide how much to jump in to meet student needs. Often, veteran teachers will suspect that the new practice is really an old one that's been *relabeled*. As Elmore (2011) notes, teachers "demonstrate an amazingly resilient capacity to relabel existing practices with whatever ideas are currently in vogue" (p. 36). He suggests that by relabeling practices or using new and popular terms, educators believe they are actually changing their practices and thinking.

One contemporary example of relabeling can be seen in today's popular personalization and differentiation movements, which are really modern adaptations of Helen Parkhurst's individualized "Dalton Plan." In the 1920s, Parkhurst founded the Dalton School in New York City, using the plan to monitor the *personal* progress of each student. Today, throughout the world, there are schools dedicated to practicing the philosophy of individualized learning embedded in the Dalton Plan (see www.daltoninternational.org). As Pulliam and Van Patten (1999) remind us, "The idea of students participating in choosing what and when they would learn goes back to Parkhurst" (p. 189). In fact, it goes back even further: Parkhurst learned about individualization and cooperative work by studying and working in Italy with Maria Montessori.

Proponents of today's personalization and differentiation movements should take pride in linking their practices with Parkhurst and Montessori's pioneering work. The connections give them added credibility. (For today's educators, tweaking Parkhurst's personalization strategies might include accentuating student voice and empowerment—it's one thing to personalize instruction and provide targeted feedback, quite another to facilitate and promote student ownership of learning.)

Education Reform and Historical Amnesia

A fair examination of the history of American education dispels the argument of some reformers that there was ever a "Golden Age" of higher standards that today's schools are failing to live up to—a narrative entrenched at least since the release of *A Nation at Risk* (U.S. Department of Education, 1983). As Ravitch (2000) notes, "It is impossible to find a period in the 20th century in which education reformers, parents, and the citizenry were satisfied with the schools" (p. 13); Tyack and Cuban (1995) make the point that reformers of all political stripes can find events from the past to support or reject current school practices.

Studying the history of education can also help practitioners to realize that the challenges they face are not unprecedented or impossible to solve. Consider the following quote from an 1870s school critic: "The school year has become one long period of . . . cram, the object of which is to successfully pass a state's series of examinations. This leads directly to superficiality" (in Nehring, 2007, p. 427). Sound familiar? Similarly, the 1892 Committee of Ten, tasked with making recommendations to restructure U.S. secondary schools, included criticisms of elementary education with a familiar ring:

> The high school teacher finds in the pupils fresh from the grammar schools no foundation of elementary school mathematical conceptions outside of arithmetic; no acquaintance with algebraic language; and no accurate knowledge of geometrical forms. As to botany, zoology, chemistry, and physics, the minds of pupils entering the high school are ordinarily blank on these subjects. (Committee of Ten, 1894, p. 15)

The authors of the report also took a strong stand against tracking students, concluding

> that every subject which is taught at all in a secondary school should be taught in the same way and to the same extent to every pupil so long as he pursues it, no matter what the probable destination of the pupil may be, or at what point his education is to cease. (p. 17)

Obviously, citing student failures, criticizing teachers, and mandating high-stakes tests are very old games. We can do better.

Technology and Historical Amnesia

Educators planning to purchase technology resources can save millions of dollars for their districts by reading articles and visiting other schools to learn about historical successes and disappointments. Consider, for example, the conclusions of an *Education Week* article published more than 25 years ago, "Planning for Technology: Few Matching Dollars with Foresight" (West, 1989). The article examines the 1988 implementation of a technology plan at Mainland Senior High School in Daytona Beach, Florida, stimulated by a $1.5 million state grant. The school principal, Michael Osborne, reported that teachers were involved in every aspect of the plan and that arrangements were being made for them to receive professional development. The school was also retrofitting to ensure that lighting was adequate and that there were enough electrical outlets to accommodate new computers. (Today, retrofitting would more likely address issues related to bandwidth, Wi-Fi, and mobile devices). Mainland's 1988 effort was "prefaced by years of planning activities that brought together technology experts, teachers, parents, local businesses, and other members of the community."

Unlike Mainland, other schools all over the country in the 1980s were spending thousands on technology without purposeful implementation plans. In 1988, the Institute for the Transfer of Technology to Education (ITTE) reported that most U.S. school technology plans were simply reacting to outside pressures to adopt the latest trends rather than using technology to address educational challenges, stating that "seldom were the [planning] documents a statement of the kinds of ways in which a school district was going to take advantage of the technology to satisfy the educational goals it set for itself."

The story of Mainland High School and the conclusions of the ITTE report offer three important lessons for educators today: Plan thoughtfully, base technology decisions on sound pedagogy, and remember that today's problems are similar to yesterday's problems.

Success in Action: The Maker Movement

Teachers and scientists involved in the maker movement in and outside of schools have successfully capitalized on technological advances to facilitate problem solving, collaborative work, scientific thinking, meeting STEM goals, and even student tenacity and joy by supporting the designing and construction of creative physical objects. The maker movement can make a significant contribution to student success through thoughtful educational planning or flame out as a fad by failing to address suitable instructional strategies.

One excellent example of how to successfully promote and implement activities related to the maker movement can be gleaned from the work of scientists and educators at San Francisco's Exploratorium, a science, art, and human perception museum (Bevan, Petrich, & Wilkinson, 2014/2015; see www.exploratorium.edu). Over the past 40 years, museum staff have worked and partnered with more than 400,000 teachers, in 1,000 school districts, 49 states, and 23 countries. The museum stands out because its staff appreciates the work of educators, understands pedagogy, and appreciates the historical roots of the maker movement. The directors of the Exploratorium aim to create programs that support inventive but structured guided activities for students, which they believe is the best conduit for deep learning. The directors of the Exploratorium, Bevan, Petrich, and Wilkinson, cannot be accused of historical amnesia if their words are any indication:

> Making as an instructional practice has deep roots. John Dewey, Jean Piaget, John Friedrich Froebel, and Maria Montessori all promoted making as central to the process of learning. Seymour Papert … argued that the process of physically constructing an object is an

effective way for students to both develop and demonstrate understanding. The current maker movement extends and updates this
history by integrating digital tools and technologies (such as small,
low-cost microprocessors or 3-D design software) into activities
that support young people's design and construction goals. (p. 30)

Such refreshing remarks reveal a humility about the movement
often absent from reform implementation. Whereas others involved
in the maker movement have stated that now is their time in
the spotlight and they must seize it or it might not come around
again (Herold, 2014b), Bevan, Petrich, and Wilkinson note that the
research base for the movement is still relatively new and that much
documentation is still needed to assess its efficacy. They suggest
that schools should first experiment with after-school programs and
partner with museums or libraries to test maker strategies before
introducing them in class.

Bevan and colleagues describe the maker movement work of Ed
Crandall's 9th grade physics class, noting that the teacher has created
a maker space where students can design, test, and build physical
objects. The authors describe one student trying to create a swim-
mer's gill for delivering oxygen, another creating nozzles for cans
of spray-paint, and a group of students designing a device to create
and measure rainfall. All these activities stress the importance of
experimentation, prediction, data gathering, testing, and revisiting
assumptions and predictions. Because many of the jobs students
will hold in the future do not yet exist, the maker movement may be
uniquely positioned for the present moment by encouraging students
to tackle challenging problems with unpredictable outcomes head on.

Time will tell whether the maker movement has sustaining
power. But if proponents of the initiative follow the examples set by
the Exploratorium museum—a reverence for educational history, the
importance of teacher training, and thoughtful pedagogical planning—then the movement is sure to inspire students for years to come.

The Chapter Reference Guide (Figure 6) links the historical
amnesia red flag with the embracing timeless and eclectic teaching
practices guidelines, highlighting key chapter points.

FIGURE 6

Chapter Reference Guide: Historical Amnesia and Embracing Timeless and Eclectic Teaching Practices

	Red Flag: Historical Amnesia	Guideline: Embracing Timeless and Eclectic Teaching Practices
Definition	Making little or no effort to explore the historical antecedents of a proposed initiative	Implementing classical and enduring teaching strategies and avoiding either/or traps that force educators to choose one good idea over another
Big Ideas	• When practitioners ignore educational history, they lose the advantage of improving their practice by reflecting on the experiences of the past. • Educators must cautiously approach "state-of-the-art" innovations that fail to acknowledge their influences or immediate predecessors.	• Timeless practices provide guidelines and scaffolding that can strengthen new initiatives. • The "Genius of the AND" approach (Collins & Porras, 2002) encourages teachers to synthesize the best features of different ideas.
Essential Questions	• How can educators do a better job of examining the historical antecedents of current reform initiatives? • Why has the pendulum metaphor, with teachers swinging from one idea to its polar opposite, dominated thinking in education?	• How can educators sustain timeless teaching practices while also promoting credible state-of-the-art reforms? • How can educators prevent "throwing the baby out with the bathwater" when they discard old initiatives in favor of new ones?
Drawbacks and Advantages	**Drawbacks:** • Ignoring history increases the likelihood that previous mistakes will be repeated. • Underserved students, in particular, have suffered from prejudicial educational practices of the past that risk returning due to historical amnesia.	**Advantages:** • When new educators are mentored in the use of timeless practice by seasoned veterans, they are less likely to be tempted by education fads. • The "Genius of the AND" approach frees willing educators from the either/or trap.
Examples	• Failing to refine practices based on past maker movement initiatives • Procuring and using technology resources without reviewing lessons from other districts' experiences	• Socratic seminars • Synthesizing practices: Dewey's learning by doing with problem-based learning

Embracing Timeless and Eclectic Teaching Practices

> **Principle #11:** Embracing and synthesizing contrary ideas is challenging, but it reminds us that complexity and paradox are part of life.

I would have been a better teacher and principal if I had not so often viewed new reforms as either/or dilemmas—adopting a *new* idea meant dropping an *old* idea. (See Appendix D for a list of common either/or dilemmas related to education.) The aha came when I read about Collins and Porras's (2002) "Genius of the AND" discussed briefly at the top of this chapter. They noted that successful companies were simultaneously "philosophical, visionary, futuristic AND superb [at] daily execution, 'nuts and bolts'" (p. 44).

The "Genius of the AND"

As Collins and Porras (2002) put it, "Tyranny of the OR" pushes people into different corners, while the "Genius of the AND" celebrates paradox by embracing *all* corners. They quote F. Scott Fitzgerald: "The test of a first-rate intelligence is the ability to hold two opposed ideas in the mind at the same time, and still retain the ability to function" (p. 45). Embracing the "Genius of the AND" allows us to sidestep the narratives of polarization that plague education. An example of the "Genius of the AND" in action would be a typical flipped lesson, which might include a lecture or demonstration video that students watch outside of class *and* in-class conferencing with students.

Tyack and Cuban (1995), too, reject the either/or approach, in their case in favor of what they refer to as *tinkering*. Their in-depth study of past reform efforts has led them to recommend change by "tinkering [as] one way of preserving what is valuable and reworking what is not" (p. 5) and "graft[ing] thoughtful reforms onto what is healthy in the present system" (p. 133).

It's important to note that neither the "Genius of the AND" nor the tinkering approach means implementing ideas one after the other but, rather, synthesizing the best bits from all of them. In the past, the either/or approach too often meant throwing the baby out with the bathwater, with many good ideas vanishing when the newest "answer" surfaced. What we should be doing is teaching creativity *and* structure, content *and* imagination. The "Genius of the AND" extends to larger structural realities, too: Instead of seeing the school and the community as separate and distinct entities, stakeholders might create a synthesis resulting in full-service community schools and centers. For example, the Harlem Children's Zone offers children a comprehensive academic program *and* health care, meals, and after-school opportunities for students and their families.

The "Genius of the AND" approach is well suited for teachers who are comfortable with synthesis, complexity, and eclecticism—the kind who might, over the course of several weeks, engage students in cooperative learning, lecture, flipped instruction, individual formative assessment conferences, a question-and-answer review using mobile devices, solo and group presentations, class discussions, video conferencing with students in another country, and a community service field trip. This kind of teacher, most often a seasoned practitioner, is using *time-tested truths* (Ravitch, 2000)—strategies that have been proven successful over the years—to support and help students succeed. Timeless practices must not be lost in the race to remain on the cutting edge. Among such practices are manifestations of *character*—empathy for children, passion, dedication, humor, capacity for growth, and a caring nature—that make all the difference in the world. Indeed, Marx (2014) and Ravitch (2000) remind us that successful teaching *begins with caring and well-educated teachers.* (Of course, context can never be omitted from the equation; an exemplary teacher in one setting may have little success in another. The most comprehensive list of exemplary practices and teacher qualities will never cover all possible circumstances.)

Timeless Practice: An Eclectic Approach to Teaching

Skillful teachers continuously assess student needs, curriculum goals, and the best ways to approach different topics before employing specific teaching strategies from a rich repertoire of choices (Cuban,

2013; Gardner, 2011; Ravitch, 2000; Wiggins & McTighe, 1998). "Where students bring different motivations, varied interests, and a range of aptitudes and abilities—no one way of teaching would ever suffice," writes Cuban (2013). "A broad repertoire of teaching activities and tasks has a better chance of working than any doctrine pedagogy" (p. 181). Educators limit the possibilities of meeting student needs if they believe there is only one "right" way to teach or one type of "good" school.

Timeless Practice: Sound Lesson Design

Juggling a variety of teaching strategies is challenging, but fortunately there are elements of effective lessons that can serve as scaffolds for practitioners. Of course, experienced teachers know that every lesson does not include every basic element—a key point, often overlooked during summative observations, drilled home to me one summer when I studied with Madeline Hunter and found myself immersed in phrases like "checking for understanding" and "guided practice." Mike Schmoker (2011a) succinctly describes key lesson elements built on Hunter's ideas:

- **Clear learning objectives** that describe the "topic, skill, or concept selected from the agreed-upon curriculum" (p. 53).
- **Teaching/modeling/demonstrating**—"often variations on lecture or direct teaching—explaining, demonstrating, instructing" (p. 53).
- **Guided practice** during which, "at brief intervals, the teacher must allow students [at times in pairs and groups] to practice or apply what has been taught or modeled" (pp. 53–54). Teachers should circulate around the room during guided practice to see how well students are grasping new information.
- **Checks for understanding/formative assessment** that provide teachers with feedback to tweak and adjust their lessons. Schmoker notes that "this step . . . is still seldom implemented with consistency" (p. 54).

A critical point: to succeed with inquiry lessons, problem-based learning, or major "discovery" activities, students still need to be taught the content knowledge necessary to creatively explore new terrain (Bransford et al., 2000). As Riley (2016) notes, solving problems and "thinking well requires knowing facts that help us make sense of new information" (p. 36).

Gabriel (2016) reminds us that

> a teacher's observable practices are only as good as their awareness of student needs and strengths, their funds of professional knowledge, their intentional use of that knowledge, and *their responsiveness to dynamic interactions of students, texts, and activities in their particular classroom context.* (italics added; p. 52)

This kind of wisdom takes time to develop. In a study of math achievement data from urban districts, Papay and Kraft (2016) estimated that math teachers can still improve their teaching performance by approximately 35 percent *even after 10 years,* especially if they receive regular professional development. Papay and Kraft specifically cite peer collaboration, teacher evaluation (with detailed feedback), job training (e.g., coaching), and organizational support as critical levers of professional growth. On the corporate side, Zenger and Folkman (2002) stress that classroom training, regardless of how powerful, cannot match on-the-job experience, which accounts for about 80 percent of the learning needed to succeed.

Timeless Practice: A Rich, Well-Rounded Curriculum

According to Munson (2011), "The nations whose students score at the top of international education tests share a dedication to providing their students with a comprehensive education across the liberal arts and sciences" (p. 12). And yet, many continue to assume that focusing on high-stakes reading and writing tests will make the United States more competitive on international tests. The truth is that reading comprehension improves when students engage with a more rather than less balanced curriculum. Citing the research of Daniel Willingham, Munson writes that "when we fail to teach students all subjects, their ability to read falters. . . . Prior knowledge across subjects enables students to comprehend" (p. 13).

The litmus-test question is, Are the students I'm working with receiving the kind of education I'd want for my own children? Most parents want their kids exposed to a broad range of subjects and experiences including history, science, math, reading and literature, civics, foreign language, the performing and visual arts, and physical education (and the team-building experiences sports can yield), with state-of-the-art technology integrated in class. Participating in school plays, for example, offers students a wealth of skills to prepare them for success in life: They get to collaborate with groups, experience the pressure of performance, see firsthand how hard work leads to success, take on a variety of responsibilities, analyze a plot, interpret a character's actions, and memorize lines.

Timeless Practice: Modeling Democracy in the Classroom and Community

Among all the pressures to implement the latest reforms and use new technologies, educators can easily overlook the most enduring purpose of schooling in the United States: to perpetuate democratic ideals through a system that provides a first-rate education for every student. Possibly the most successful and consequential progressive reform ever implemented in the United States is the integration of schools, which embodies the essence of a democracy: equal opportunity for all (Hannah-Jones, 2016). At the same time, continuing political efforts to roll back school integration, perpetuated by the injustice of residential segregation, is a major reason for the persistent opportunity gap between students of color and their peers.

Ferrero (2011) laments the lack of enthusiasm for history and civics in U.S. schools. He sees civics as "equipping students with the knowledge and skills necessary to be good citizens" (p. 23). If electing leaders is a fundamental responsibility of democracies, civics education should prioritize stimulating student interest in the electoral process. Only 58 percent of eligible voters exercised their right in the 2016 presidential election, with a much lower rate for state and local elections (Regan, 2016). Social media is another reason to teach civics in a democracy: The proliferation of false information on the internet requires students to know how to discriminate between fact and fiction.

Educators can model civic principles by enthusiastically interacting with, and listening to, colleagues, students, parents, and the community. The broader community needs to see that schools operate entirely in accordance with democratic principles. Professional learning communities, faculty meetings, student body meetings, and parent association gatherings all offer plenty of opportunities for democratic action. Darling-Hammond (2010) notes that a strategy with particular success among underserved students is to "forge positive connections to their communities and families" (p. 162). When students interact with adults to create meaningful outcomes, they learn lessons about empowerment and contributing to society. The middle and high school students who participated in the strategic planning process at the Singapore American School (see p. 114), for example, developed skills related to confidence and agency that will serve them well long after graduation.

Leading as Caring Teachers

Experienced teachers mentoring new ones will often begin by citing the importance of fostering a caring classroom, displaying empathy, and having high expectations for all students. Though new recruits might think of these as secondary issues, over time they inevitably find that they are key elements of lesson planning and disciplinary effectiveness. Brandon Busteed (2014), executive director of Gallup Education, reports that "when Gallup polled Americans and asked them to describe the best teacher they ever had, the most common word used was 'caring'" (p. 26).

Cognitive science research also supports the central importance of caring. Students are more motivated to learn when teachers "praise productive student efforts" that tap into both ability and intelligence (Riley, 2016, p. 36). Caring teachers employ personalization strategies by affirming students' cultural origins and learning about their strengths, weaknesses, interests, sources of motivation, home lives, social pressures, hopes, and dreams. Finally, caring teachers notice and embrace working with *all* students from all backgrounds (including those in many classrooms who feel invisible because they rarely make waves).

✓ Action Checklist to Avoid Historical Amnesia and Promote Embracing Timeless and Eclectic Teaching Practices

When considering reform initiatives during collaboration:

_____ 1. Resolve to examine the historical lineage of proposed initiatives and how they affect students before moving toward implementation.

_____ 2. Embrace relabeled or revisited reforms if they have been tweaked to better serve students in the classroom.

_____ 3. Use Collins and Porras's "Genius of the AND" approach to synthesize the best ideas from different reform initiatives.

_____ 4. Support both innovative reforms _and_ timeless practices—and the synthesis of both—to meet the classroom needs of students.

_____ 5. Advance the success of digital tools and digital learning strategies by first targeting instructional goals and appropriate pedagogical strategies.

_____ 6. Champion democratic classrooms and schools that promote collaboration and critical thinking, where antibullying practices are modeled and every student is treasured.

_____ 7. Promote a comprehensive, well-rounded curriculum (including technology and arts components) that offers the same opportunities to both affluent and historically underserved students.

_____ 8. Support new and seasoned faculty by promoting the timeless practices and qualities of caring, eclectic teaching, sound lesson design, and a rich and well-rounded curriculum.

Chapter Reflections: Questions and Activities

Please feel free to adapt these questions and activities to meet individual or interactive group goals.

Questions

1. Reflect on your elementary, middle, or high school years. What were some of the popular teaching strategies, programs, and resources you remember? Do you incorporate any of them into your practice today?

2. Did you enjoy school as a child or adolescent? Were you successful? Did you *feel* successful? Did you feel you were treated fairly? Have these experiences affected your present work? If yes, how?

3. Jot down two to three educational reforms that are currently popular. Do you think they are completely new? Relabeled practices—old wine in new bottles? Hybrid practices? Share your thoughts with colleagues.

4. Can the "Genius of the AND" approach help educators tackle issues that your district or school is currently dealing with? How?

5. Review the section on embracing timeless and eclectic teaching practices. Do you agree with the practices discussed? What would you add or remove?

6. Based on reading this chapter, what new insights, ahas, or concerns do you have?

7. What beliefs has this chapter reaffirmed?

8. What additional questions need to be asked?

Interactive Activity: Finding Common Ground

1. Create groups of two to four members. Members individually should consider two programs or practices, past or present— one that they support and one that they oppose. If possible, the two reforms should relate to a similar topic (e.g., two reading pro-

grams). Jot down a few notes describing the purpose of the initiatives and what implementation looks like in a school or district.

2. Share your ideas with other group members, describing the contrasts between the two initiatives.

3. Using the "Genius of the AND" strategy, take a few minutes on your own to try synthesizing the best elements of the two initiatives. Is there common ground? Can the ideas be fused? Can elements from the two initiatives coexist in the same school?

4. Share how you managed the challenge of synthesizing the ideas. What difficulties did you encounter? After everyone has shared, discuss the benefits and any downsides of the "Genius of the AND" approach.

5. Discuss any takeaways.

The Business "Solution" and Championing and Empowering the Underserved

---

Many companies these days are shifting from management by objectives to leading by values.

Bill George

During much of the 20th century, educators were greatly influenced by Frederick Taylor's principles of Scientific Management, which had transformed productivity and factory work. Although Taylor is not well known today, many management experts believe that his influence on the U.S. factory system was greater than Henry Ford's. Taylor viewed the workplace as a closed, efficient, hierarchical system, in which each facet of a laborer's day could be quantified and refined, undeterred by outside environmental factors. He valued lockstep adherence to group behavior in the factory, dismissing worker individuality.

"This is an age of efficiency," said Dartmouth professor James McConaughy in 1918. "In the eyes of the public no indictment of a school can be more severe than to say it is inefficient" (Hanson, 2003). The reliance of today's school accountability movement on data, state testing, standards, and teacher evaluation as the sole measures of success parallels Taylor's management work; accountability and group efficiency go hand in hand. Of course, accountability is important—although NCLB legislation proved wanting, the law did remind the public that schools have urgent problems, including unacceptable dropout rates and achievement and opportunity gaps that adversely affect historically underserved students. However, the notion that Taylor's business principles will fix U.S. schools is a red flag.

Every school is a contextually unique and complex open system, part of a community—not an isolated silo that can be fixed solely through internal accountability and structural changes. Accountability strategies have not significantly affected test scores, social-emotional learning concerns, or the interaction between individual students and teachers (Fullan, 2011; Ladd, Noguera, Reville, & Starr, 2016). Because schools are open systems, partnering between the school and community is critical to address the educational needs of underserved students. Students are not just statistics; the ASCD Whole Child approach stresses the importance of valuing each student's strengths and role as a global citizen—qualities that are very difficult to quantify. Guidelines on these issues will be addressed later in this chapter.

As noted in Chapter 2, the "No Excuses" approach, offered by some reformers, provides an excuse and exit ramp for society to disregard its responsibility to schools by failing to acknowledge how much school success is related to environmental factors. Reality tells us, however, that local environmental factors have a great deal to do with school success. Lewis and Burd-Sharps (2016) examined the school choice program in New York City and found that regardless of where students attended public high school (charters were included), the overwhelming determinant of whether students graduated in four years was the neighborhood they called home— much more so than race, ethnicity, and gender. Regardless of where they went to high school, more than 95 percent of students from wealthier city neighborhoods graduated—compared to 61 percent of their peers from economically disadvantaged neighborhoods. The report concluded:

> Far too many young people from low-income black and Latino neighborhoods in the Bronx and central Brooklyn are winding up in high schools with low graduation rates, going to school mostly with other teens who share their socioeconomic disadvantages. . . . Children living in poverty in the United States face tremendous challenges—from ill health and hunger to exposure to trauma and social exclusion. . . . Expecting teachers, principals, and school administrators to right society's most serious wrongs flies in the face of common sense; to blame them for failing to do so is unfair. . . . *[M]aking educational equality a reality requires investments in children, families, and communities far beyond the education sector.* (italics added; Lewis & Burd-Sharps, 2016, pp. 11–12)

The Business "Solution" (or, Comparing Apples to Oranges)

Principle #12: Schools are not factories, and students are not merchandise.

When I was a child, I shopped with my parents (as infrequently as possible) at the Alexander's Department Store on the corner of Fordham Road and the Grand Concourse in the Bronx. A prized possession in those days was a pair of Converse All-Stars basketball sneakers, but they were expensive. Fortunately, every once in a while, Alexander's had a basement sale where "Cons" were about half price. The discount only applied to sneakers that were slightly damaged (maybe the sewing pattern was a little off or a couple of eyelets were missing). The damaged sneakers were referred to as "irregulars" and even had the word "irregular" stamped on them. Colloquially, we called the damaged and discounted merchandise "seconds." Regardless, they were still "Cons," and we were just glad to own a pair.

Businesses can sell damaged merchandise at a discount, give items away to a food bank, or dispose of the merchandise altogether.

Schools, however, cannot possibly refer to students with challenging issues as "damaged goods." Human beings are not "seconds" to be discarded or sold in the basement at a discounted price. Students who begin school having experienced trauma or serious hardship need the school's help to overcome it. Yet educators, often pressured by corporate and political forces, feel compelled to define success solely through bottom-line statistics that rarely present a full portrait of the challenges public schools face.

Ironically, many *businesses* are reexamining the traditional definition of business success. Collins and Porras (2002) note that visionary companies exercise "purpose beyond profit" (p. 44). (For example, Starbucks offers a full health care package for employees who work at least 20 hours a week and partners with Arizona State University to help employees graduate college.)

There do exist business concepts that schools should embrace, such as collaboration. As Senge (1992) notes, successful learning organizations are not made up of silos but, rather, of interrelated parts. For systems thinking to work, all members of an organization need to trust each other, take pride in their profession and capacity to grow, and recognize their mutual responsibility to a set of common goals.

Senge's ideas appear to be alive and well among the teachers in Finland. Writing about the successful reform efforts in his home nation, Sahlberg describes a landscape quite different from that in the United States:

> Teachers compare what they do in a primary school to the work that doctors do in medical clinics. . . . Unlike nations that have bureaucratic accountability systems that make teachers feel threatened, overcontrolled, and undervalued, teaching in Finland is a very sophisticated profession, where teachers feel they can truly exercise the skills they have learned in the university. Test-based accountability is replaced by trust-based responsibility and inspiration for human development. (in Darling-Hammond & Rothman, 2015, pp. 37–38)

Although U.S. society may be a long way from treating teachers with the respect displayed in Finland, there are positive signs. The

2015 ESSA eliminated the punitive adequate yearly progress measures, NCLB-mandated reading and math proficiency goals of 100 percent, the coupling of teacher evaluations to student test scores, and the linkage of federal grants to the CCSS. These are hopeful signals to state governments that teachers should be trusted to be in the best position to make curriculum, instruction, assessment, and professional development decisions with local stakeholders.

How Did We Get Here?

In 1916, Ellwood P. Cubberley, the dean of Stanford's Graduate School of Education, stated: "Our schools are, in a sense, factories in which the raw products (children) are to be shaped and fashioned to meet the various demands of life" (in Hanson, 2003, p. 22). Until the Wall Street crash of 1929, industrial leaders wielded great influence over many aspects of society, including schools. Not surprisingly, business concepts often lose their luster with the public after an economic downturn. This was certainly the case during the Great Depression, when the focus of Scientific Management on *task* behavior lost some popularity. Newer approaches soon emerged advocated by the likes of Mary Parker Follett and Elton Mayo, emphasizing *individual potential, human relations, collaboration,* and *democratic principles.* Today, there are many visible examples in education of these relationship-oriented concepts, including professional learning communities, co-teaching, edcamps, and school-community programs such as the Comer Process and the Harlem Children's Zone. Certainly, success in most situations depends on effectively exercising *both* task and relationship behaviors.

Darling-Hammond (2010) believes that the historical legacy of Taylor's factory model in schools has limited teacher professional development and collaborative opportunities to share expertise. But why have business concepts been so influential among educators in the first place? According to Peck and Reitzug (2012), business elites, elected officials, and policymakers shape educational management strategies and policies because they "occupy strategic positions (e.g., school boards, civic forums) that afford them immense influence to ensure that ideas developed in and for their sector hold sway over the education sector" (p. 358). Peck and Reitzug suggest that educational leadership professors, consultants, foundation supporters, and school administrative associations are the "fashion setters" that disseminate the business concepts to school practitioners and principal programs. Their analysis, which covered four decades of school reforms, thought-provokingly suggests that when popular concepts are discarded from the business world (e.g., management by objectives, total quality management, turnarounds), they reemerge in education. Peck and Reitzug suggest that educators have embraced "fading business management concepts," looking outside for solutions "in the name of K–12 school reform" (pp. 352, 375). Their study was influenced by Tyack and Cuban's (1995) observations that business-oriented school reformers often use economic terms such as "productivity, market, customers, restructuring, payoff, rollout, and total quality management. The terms have changed over the years, but not the impulse to emulate business" (p. 112).

Peck and Reitzug (2012) optimistically suggest that when educators recognize how dependent they've been on these borrowed management ideas, they'll move to develop leadership concepts more appropriate for schools. This will not be easy, as business concepts dominate U.S. society, and some of them even show promise if properly modified for use in schools. To move forward, Peck and Reitzug challenge educators to develop *contextually appropriate leadership reform strategies* that reject outdated business concepts. They encourage educators to engage in "collegial dialogue," seeking "real and locally sourced innovation that prioritizes and attends to the unique circumstances of leading schools" (p. 375).

The Hybrid Approach

A hybrid approach certainly holds promise if the best ideas from education and business can be joined to address local challenges. For example, Collins's (2005) advice to continuously build organizational capacity makes sense to both education and business professionals. As he puts it: "Greatness is an inherently dynamic process, not an endpoint. The moment you think of yourself as great, your slide toward mediocrity will have already begun" (p. 9). Similarly, Darling-Hammond and Rothman (2015), in their analysis of high-performing school systems from around the world, conclude that each system (e.g., Singapore, Finland, and Ontario, Canada) *started to improve by first recognizing that it needed to do better.* Adhering to a hybrid approach, Singapore, Finland, and Ontario all applied Senge's systems thinking approach, stressing that learning organizations are comprised of coherent and interrelated parts. When recommending reforms for U.S. schools, Darling-Hammond and Rothman note that high-performing nations have in common "*systems* for teacher and leader development. They include multiple components, not just a single policy, and these components are intended to be coherent and complementary, to support the overall goal" (italics in original; p. 76). The goal is for each nation and school to have first-rate principals and teachers in place.

Darling-Hammond and Rothman stress that the systems approach does not preclude attacking specific levers based on a school's perceived weak points (e.g., the imperative to recruit better-qualified teachers in high-risk urban schools). But a crucial point of systems thinking is recognizing that each lever is part of a larger whole. Recruiting excellent teachers is only a first step. Other critical leverage points include treating teachers as professionals, recognizing their accomplishments, equitably allocating resources and teachers, and preparing instructional leaders. (On a related note, as a school principal, I sometimes had to remind myself to pay attention to outstanding veteran teachers by noting and affirming their accomplishments. New and struggling teachers are not the only ones who welcome encouragement and deserve professional development. Exceptional experienced teachers should never be taken for granted.)

Darling-Hammond and Rothman emphasize that many of the systemic elements in high-performing international school systems are also everyday goals for U.S. school districts, with many doing quite well in these areas (e.g., recruiting excellent teachers, equitably allocating resources). The difficult part is prioritizing and discerning which contextual leverage point to address first and recognizing that once progress is made in one area, other parts of the system need to be addressed.

"There Is a Price to Pay for Arrogance"

In *True North* (2007), Bill George profiles Kevin Sharer, whose "gut-wrenching" experiences and mistakes while trying to move up the corporate ladder taught him the importance of humility and patience: "I learned that whether you are right or not, there is a price to pay for arrogance" (pp. 36–37). Sharer, who eventually became CEO of the biotech company Amgen, points to the importance of loving your work and listening to experienced company voices as crucial elements to success.

Respect for professional educators and their local challenges must be the starting point for corporate reformers who want to successfully work with schools. Arrogance, the carrot-and-stick approach, and denigrating teachers do not work. Fullan (2011) writes that teacher professionalism is undermined when accountability is used as a leading driver of change: "A focus on accountability uses standards, assessment, rewards and punishment as its core drivers" (p. 8). Teacher merit-pay programs, for example, have achieved mixed results at best. According to Darling-Hammond and Rothman (2015), "A closely watched, rigorously conducted study in Nashville found that providing bonuses to teachers for improvements in student test scores did not produce higher levels of student learning" (p. 25). Moreover, many teachers are insulted by the notion that monetary incentives will affect their dedication and performance.

For business concepts to work in schools, corporate-reform purists need to recognize that modifying their ideas after listening to local voices increases the chances of success. Michael McGill (2014), a former New York State Superintendent of the Year from Scarsdale, New York, complains that the "corporate model" of education "assumes de facto [that] education is a test score. It then depends on a tightly coupled system of control and audit to drive scores higher. Higher scores must mean education is improving."

A LESSON LEARNED

Honor the Wisdom of Experienced Professionals

In April of my first year as principal of the Singapore American School, I was reviewing the file for the June graduation ceremony. While reading, I took notes on changes I wanted to institute for the ceremony, largely based on my previous experience as a high school principal.

A couple of days later, I met with the school's athletic and activities director, Bob Connor, who had worked at the Singapore American School for a decade and coordinated the ceremony logistics. I was fairly pleased with the changes I was going to institute for the ceremony and looked forward to sharing my ideas with Bob. After listening to my proposals, he responded.

"Harvey," he said, "you have never attended our graduation ceremony, so you have no idea how successful it is. This is the first time we have even talked about the event. Are we going to make these decisions together?"

I immediately realized that Bob was right. I had been a principal for 11 years, yet had made a rookie mistake out of arrogance—and maybe a desire to show how much I already knew. Embarrassed, I told Bob that he was right, withdrew most of my suggestions, and asked him to review last year's graduation ceremony sequence. We brainstormed for a few more minutes and made a couple of minor changes.

In the end, the graduation was impressive. Bob did a great job, and I was grateful to be part of the ceremony. The whole process was a valuable learning experience. What's more, now that I had participated in the ceremony I had some credibility and could make suggestions based on experience rather than arrogance.

Embracing compromise with educators, by moving from control to trust, signals a desire to listen and learn how school change works.

Rami Madani and David Neudorf (2015), administrators at the International School of Kuala Lumpur, note that data-driven curriculum decisions that are solely dependent on tests scores often end up being *deficit-driven,* with educators, board members, and parents examining only what students and teachers are doing wrong. Thus, it makes sense to use multiple measures to assess student progress. Meier suggests that "school should be 'data-informed,' not data driven" (in Ravitch, 2010, p. 229).

Transformational Versus Instructional Leadership

Russakoff (2015a) identified the term "transformation" as the word of choice among corporate reformers in her study of Newark, New Jersey, schools. She notes that "Teach for America promised *'transformational teachers'*; New Leaders for New Schools, *'transformational'* principals; the Broad Center, *superintendents 'with transformational skill and will'* who would enact *'transformational, sustainable and replicable reforms'*" (pp. 68–69). Hattie (2015) contrasts the term *transformational leader* with *instructional leader*, concluding, "The push for transformational leadership has come from the business community and from policymakers who are looking to 'transform' schools, and it has led to higher status for the business lookalikes within and outside school" (p. 38). Summarizing the meta-analysis research of Robinson, Lloyd, and Rowe on school leaders who characterize themselves as transformational or instructional leaders, Hattie notes that the effect size ("a standard method to measure the strength or magnitude of a relationship") of instructional leadership was .42, while the transformational leadership effect size was considerably lower at .11—"a huge difference" (p. 38).

Transformational school leaders accentuate teacher autonomy, vision, and school goals. Instructional leadership emphasizes individual students, classroom observations, professional development, feedback, and a culture that supports teaching and learning. Can an educator be both a transformational *and* an instructional leader? Why not? The best thing to do is to take a hybrid approach, integrating the best features of instructional and transformational leadership—but always starting with the premise that schools are not factories.

The Chapter Reference Guide (Figure 7) links the business "solution" red flag with the championing and empowering the underserved guidelines, highlighting key chapter points.

FIGURE 7

Chapter Reference Guide: The Business "Solution" and Championing and Empowering the Underserved

	Red Flag: The Business "Solution"	Guideline: Championing and Empowering the Underserved
Definition	Strategies based on Scientific Management principles—bureaucratic and data-driven group efficiency, students as merchandise, and schools as closed systems to be managed without addressing outside social, political, safety, and economic issues related to the community	Affirming the right of each student to receive a superior education that values equity, equality, excellence, and the positive qualities that individual children bring to school; rejecting an approach to learning that discounts the effects of social and economic forces on schools
Big Ideas	• Student, teacher, and school success is based solely on objective group accountability measures related to standards, high-stakes testing, and teacher evaluation. • Teachers are motivated to improve their practice through monetary incentives (e.g., merit pay) and supervisory evaluation strategies that emphasize adverse consequences rather than professional development.	• Schools and society must do more to promote the nation's democratic principles of equality, equity, and excellence. • Underserved students and communities can be empowered through culturally responsive teaching strategies and by accepting community stakeholders as decision-making partners.
Essential Questions	• Why are business management concepts so appealing to educators? • How can the gap be narrowed between those who view schools as closed systems to be fixed internally and those who believe social safety net issues are critical to school improvement?	• How can schools include the voices of underserved students and act so that they are not disadvantaged by reforms and school policies? • What communication strategies need to be implemented so that every student and family, regardless of background, feels comfortable in and around the district or school?
Drawbacks and Advantages	**Drawbacks:** • When student success is based solely on numbers, teaching and learning is limited, and qualitative individual success is disregarded (e.g., social-emotional learning). • Underserved students are more likely to receive "drill and kill" work that targets high-stakes tests at the expense of enrichment.	**Advantages:** • Using culturally responsive and strength-based teaching practices increases the potential for student success. • Reaching out and respecting diverse families fortifies the school-family bond and, importantly, each student's connection to school.
Examples	• The "No Excuses" narrative • Posting teacher evaluation rankings in newspapers	• Students serving as translators and guides during back-to-school nights • Engaging in home visits and fostering wraparound school services

Championing and Empowering the Underserved

Principle #13: To level the equity playing field, underserved students must be empowered and given voice to succeed in school and beyond.

Because poor and historically underrepresented students often do not have the political clout to be heard, school staff and community advocates must help to amplify their voices until local empowerment occurs. Practitioners need to ask themselves whether reforms under consideration have the potential to hurt any particular group of students. After reviewing two centuries of school reform, Nehring (2007) concluded that tough questions need to be addressed to overcome the advantage that "favored groups" have enjoyed: "Who gains from this decision? Who loses? Would I accept this loss for my own child" (p. 432)?

Consider the following facts about students from underserved communities (ASCD, 2015c; Berliner & Glass, 2014b; Darling-Hammond, 2010; Mondale & Patton, 2001):

• They have less experienced teachers and fewer resources both in and out of school.

• They are more likely to be held accountable than affluent students for their high-stakes test scores and are more likely to be adversely affected by decisions made about school placement, gifted-and-talented class placement, and graduation based on their scores.

• They are adversely affected by inequities related to school financial issues and high school opportunities (ASCD, 2015c):

   –Twenty-three states spend less per pupil in poor districts than in affluent districts.

   –The teacher turnover rate in high-poverty schools is 50 percent higher than in affluent schools.

   –Only one in three students who spend the majority of their youth in poverty graduate high school.

   –One-third the number of AP courses are offered in schools where 75 percent or more of the students live in poverty.

Students who are raised with privilege have a social and economic safety net. If they are at risk of failing in high school, or if they need to raise their SAT, ACT, or AP scores, their parents can afford tutors. If they get in trouble with the law, their parents can hire the best lawyers. Privileged students get a second and third chance when they make mistakes.

The contrast with students from underserved communities is stark. These students are much more likely to drop out of high school—and 75 percent of prison inmates are high school dropouts. As Alexander (2012) notes, "The young men who go to prison rather than college face a lifetime of closed doors, discrimination, and ostracism" (p. 190). Kuhn (2014) theorizes that U.S. society is much more comfortable talking about the disappointing graduation rates and achievement gaps of these students than "attributing the conditions of poor Americans to our social policies and historical choices" (p. 123).

When the school successes of Finland are highlighted, it should be stressed that the poverty rate in the United States is *four times* as high (Jennings, 2015). A 2013 report from the U.S. Department of Education notes that the U.S. "poverty rate for school-age children—currently more than 22 percent—is twice the OECD average. . . . We are an outlier in how we concentrate those children . . . which only magnifies poverty's impact and makes high achievement that much harder" (Jennings, 2015).

Educators, parents, and community stakeholders must ask questions about the effects of testing and intervene when tests discriminate against underserved groups. The current use and history of high-stakes tests remains disheartening. In the early 20th century, "reformers" in France used the IQ tests developed by Alfred Binet to help French schools *remove students who scored poorly* so they could "receive special services" (Berliner & Glass, 2014b, p. 235). This deficit-based approach—measuring perceived weaknesses instead of strengths—is based on the assumption that intelligence is fixed throughout one's life. Berliner and Glass maintain that the cultural bias they believe is inherent in high-stakes tests helps "explain why low-income and minority students often are under-represented in gifted-and-talented programs and over-represented in special education programs" (p. 235).

Federal laws require public schools to provide a free and appropriate education for all students and to offer special services for those with diagnosed disabilities. These services are not a privilege but a *right*. The 6.5 million special education students in the United States and their parents should feel welcome as soon as they open the front door of a public school. When I served as a principal, I knew that my attendance at individualized education plan (IEP) meetings sent a message of support to the students, their parents, and the staff helping meet the students' special needs. As an equity issue, schools must be committed to the services and expectations described on the IEP document and recognize that the document is a contract and commitment to the student (Robbins & Alvy, 2014b). It's worth noting that poor and minority students are overrepresented in special education classes (Berliner & Glass, 2014b)—an alarming fact all teachers must work to change.

Success in Action: Julian Nava

Mondale and Patton (2001) tell the story of Julian Nava, a former member of the Los Angeles Board of Education who experienced the effects of bias against students of Mexican descent as a child. "By the 1930s," note Mondale and Patton, "two-thirds of the Mexican American students in Los Angeles were classified as slow learners, and even mentally retarded, on the basis of I.Q. tests given as early as kindergarten" (p. 104). Like his older brother, Henry, Julian attended Roosevelt High School in Los Angeles. Although he wanted to take college prep classes, he was forced instead to take vocational courses such as carpentry by teachers who thought he wasn't smart enough for the former. Henry was in the Navy Medical Corps during World War II and noticed that the most dangerous jobs went to the servicemen with the lowest levels of schooling. Worried that Julian might one day face these dangers, Henry urged the school guidance counselor to let his little brother into the college prep program. The counselor refused. Julian recalled,

> I remember that Henry was a weightlifter and Navy uniforms are very tight fitting and so he had very broad shoulders and big biceps, and he looked just awesome in his Navy uniform. And he leaned over the desk and told the counselor, "You didn't hear me. Julian is going to take college prep courses." And [to me] he said, "And you are going to pass these, aren't you?" And I said yes. A good Mexican boy always says "yes" to his older brother. (pp. 107–110)

Julian would go on to earn a doctorate in history from Harvard University. While serving on the L.A. school board, he helped to end IQ testing in the city. In 1979, President Jimmy Carter appointed Nava as the U.S. ambassador to Mexico. Reflecting on his experiences growing up, Ambassador Nava stated, "We will never know how many Doctor Salks or Pablo Casals or Picassos have been lost because children from minority groups were not inspired or challenged and given the chance to show what they've got" (Mondale & Patton, 2001, p. 113).

Henry and Julian Nava's story reveals the influence of school guidance counselors. Counselors place students in various classes or programs that can open or close pathways to college and career opportunities. These include AP, honors, and regular classes in math, science, social studies, English, and modern language; career and technical education pathways; and important requirements and electives in the arts, physical education, and computer science. In most public schools, each counselor serves hundreds of students, so it's imperative for teachers, administrators, and family members to advocate for the needs of individual students.

Although Julian's success is inspiring and attests to how schools (and siblings) can change lives, it is still only one story. Too often, an inspirational story is used to reinforce a narrative that says anyone with grit can overcome poverty and prejudice. But the big picture cannot be ignored, as Ravitch (2014) reports: "There is no example in which an entire school district eliminated poverty by reforming its schools or by replacing public education with privately managed charters and vouchers" (p. 225).

Advocating for Students Through Strengths: Equity, Equality, and Excellence

Yvette Jackson and Veronica McDermott, directors with the National Urban Alliance, advocate for a *"pedagogy of confidence"* that focuses on student strengths, capacity for growth, and "potential for high intellectual performance" (italics in original; quoted in Perkins-Gough, 2015, p. 15). Deficit-based approaches neglect strengths and sacrifice enrichment opportunities for remedial classes to meet minimum testing requirements. Too often, underserved students are forced to work on the "basics" to pass standardized tests, while affluent students are welcome to pursue the arts or advanced classes.

Schools and communities should focus on equity, equality, and excellence as interrelated social justice values. *Excellence* relates to high expectations for all students in subjects and programs; *equality* holds that every student should have access to the school's human, material, and program resources; and *equity* affirms and celebrates individual student differences and the need to personalize resource use in response to them. Furman (2012) urges educators to work on aggressively "identifying and undoing... oppressive and unjust practices and replacing them with more equitable, culturally appropriate ones" (p. 194). Citing Oakes, Darling-Hammond (2010) contrasts the benefits of high-track classes where teachers emphasize independent learning, higher-order thinking, and creativity with low-track classes, void of enrichment, that emphasize compliance, low-level and minimal academic skills, and behavioral management.

Promoting a Strength and Growth Approach

In an interview with Perkins-Gough (2015), Jackson and McDermott emphasize promoting teaching strategies that empower urban students by exploiting their strengths "to build underdeveloped skills, and then providing enrichment and opportunities to apply their intelligence" (p. 15). Jackson and McDermott also discuss how language about underserved students can negatively affect them and teachers' perceptions of them, such as by constantly talking about "gaps" between them and their peers. Jackson and McDermott prefer using *gap* to mean the distance between a student's present performance and his or her potential. They are also critical of the term *turnaround schools,* which they believe stigmatizes schools as hopelessly dependent on outsiders for improvement. In its place they recommend the term *schools of promise* to express their potential to transform through local agency.

In the same interview (Perkins-Gough, 2015), Jackson and McDermott provide two excellent culturally responsive teaching strategies to empower students and families:

• Have students write about their strengths: "You might have students do a personal self-assessment consisting of broad, positive categories: What are my interests, hobbies, talents? What positive adjectives describe me?" (p. 18). Students can then share their ideas with one another. This strategy is a wonderful growth opportunity for students.

• Have students serve as translators and guides at school events such as curriculum fairs, explaining their teachers' instructional practices to family members. This strategy is especially empowering for students from families that don't speak much English and has been shown to increase event attendance. This is a great way for bilingual students to be perceived as assets to the school and their peers and for teachers to see the importance of championing their potential.

Welcoming Families Through Home Visits

Another strategy to champion and empower students and parents is that of home visits. McKibben (2016) writes about how Stephanie Smith, a teacher at Oak Ridge Elementary School in Sacramento, California, built confidence with families during eight years of home visits: Some of them initially had to be convinced that the visits were not "welfare checks," but they were eventually able to develop trusting partnerships characterized by warm phone exchanges and parent visits to class. Before beginning the visits, Smith would let parents know that she was reaching out to *all* students to strengthen home-school relationships.

The Sacramento City Unified School District is actively involved with the Parent Teacher Home Visits Project (PTHVP; see www.pthvp.org), which provides teachers with compensation and professional development related to home visits. Findings from a Johns Hopkins University study indicate that when the PTHVP model is used, family school involvement increases, student attendance improves, and students are more likely to read at grade level or above. Other PTHVP strategies shared by McKibben include arranging translators for home visits, focusing the initial visit on relationships rather than academics, and developing an action plan with parents to solidify the relationship.

Teachers who do not conduct visits express concerns about safety, time constraints, compensation, training, and the overall effectiveness of the approach. (McKibben cites an ASCD survey indicating that only 24 percent of teachers use home visits to build relationships.) However, seeing students interact at home with their families about their hopes and dreams allows us to incorporate culturally responsive teaching strategies in class. Henke (2011) shares the story of Kevin Grawer, a Missouri high school principal who learned a powerful lesson about cultural sensitivity while visiting the home of a Hispanic parent in the Maplewood Richmond Heights School District. Though he initially noticed a neat stack of English-only school newsletters and notices in the home, he quickly realized that the student's parent was unable to read English at all. Grawer immediately returned to school, used Google to translate the year's newsletters and notices, and mailed the translations to the parent. Thereafter, Grawer made sure letters in Spanish went out to all Hispanic families.

Reaching Out and Respecting Diverse Families

It's important for educators to recognize that some parents, particularly in underserved communities, have unpleasant memories of school. Unfortunately, low-income parents, parents of color, and nontraditional families, especially, have too often felt voiceless and unwelcome in schools. These parents are less likely to be willing to express their opinion than parents from more privileged or conventional backgrounds.

While serving as a principal, I once had a student's father say to me on the first day of school, "I know that if I see or hear from you this year, it is not good news. I hope this is our last conversation." After that, I made it my business to contact the parent several times during the year to establish a less wary relationship. Teachers and principals should always take the first step to break the ice with a smile and a warm greeting.

According to Philip Cohen of the University of Maryland, College Park, today's households are far more diverse than they were in 1960, when 66 percent of families were headed by married heterosexual couples with the mother staying home and the father going to work; today, only 22 percent of families fit this profile, whereas "34 percent of children are now being raised in married, dual-earner households, while the remaining 44 percent are brought up by a mix of single parents, grandparents, and other caregivers" (McKibben, 2015, p. 4). Furthermore, according to a UCLA study cited by McKibben, about 3.7 million children in the United States have an LGBT parent.

McKibben suggests the following strategies that all educators can model daily to welcome diverse families:

• **Dispel assumptions.** Avoid making any assumptions about a family's makeup until you speak with the student. When you find out the particulars, adjust your practice accordingly (e.g., if the parents are separated or divorced and the student is constantly moving between two homes, speak with him or her about the logistics involved to complete homework).

• **Use inclusive language.** If possible, send forms or newsletters to families in the language they understand best. Be sensitive to parents' last names; it is better to use inclusive greetings such as "Dear Parent or Guardian" or "Dear Family."

• **Send a visible message of acceptance.** Publicize antibullying messages in meetings and in newsletters, highlight antidiscrimination policies, and promote inclusive school organizations such as the Gay-Straight Alliance Club. Showcase library books that reflect diverse families. When hiring new staff, frame interview questions to demonstrate the school's welcoming stance.

• **Listen and ask.** Embrace diverse families by listening to their stories, ask how the school can be helpful, respectfully try to gain information about students before they enter the classroom, and listen empathetically to the hopes and desires of parents.

Integrating Schools with Communities Through Partnerships and Advocacy

The Comer Process. This approach, discussed in Chapter 2, is a holistic model empowering both practitioners and parents or guardians to make decisions together and integrate school with community programs to improve the lives of students. When discussing the success of the Comer Process, Payne (2008) makes an observation both painful and hopeful: "Yes, there are parents who have been too beaten down by life in poverty to support children adequately, but there are others who aren't and just need to be challenged and supported" (p. 203). The model has allowed many parents without organizational or job market experiences to use their volunteer work in schools as a springboard to employment.

The Broader, Bolder Approach to Education. Ladd, Noguera, Reville, and Starr (2016), all cochairs of the Broader, Bolder Approach to Education campaign, optimistically suggest that the ESSA provides an opening to initiate programs that refute the "No Excuses" narrative. Heartened by the "whole child perspective" of the ESSA (primarily related to Title IV) and greater options for local decision making, Ladd and colleagues believe that "education policy in the United States has taken a turn in a new direction . . . [with policymakers recognizing] that stresses relating to student poverty—hunger, chronic illness, and in too many cases, trauma—are the key barriers to teaching and learning" (p. 22). The Broader, Bolder Approach to Education is an advocacy campaign that supports integrating school programs with community services to mitigate poverty. Informed by evidence-based research, the approach calls for local, federal, and state agencies to fulfill their responsibilities and address student needs from birth through formal schooling by expanding the concept of education and recognizing that academics is only part of educating the whole child. The campaign advocates for policy actions in the following three main areas (Broader, Bolder Approach to Education, 2016):

1. Alleviating out-of-school factors that expand the opportunity gap: Enriching early childhood experiences from birth through the age of 5; enhancing afterschool and summer opportunities; improving health and wellness policies and practices; promoting better nutrition in and out of school

2. Implementing in-school factors that narrow the opportunity gap: Providing equitable funding and resources; promoting a holistic accountability system that includes comprehensive academic, arts, health, and physical education programs and also addresses social, emotional, and civic education; ensuring all students have access to experienced teachers and effective principals; strengthening accountability for charter schools by fostering practices of the best charters through oversight frameworks, democratic and fully transparent governance, accountability of private and public funds, and "curtailing the 'push-out' of students who are hard to teach, whose families are more difficult to engage, and whose test scores will drag down school averages" (p. 7)

3. Strengthening the community to improve student outcomes: Addressing segregation and concentrated poverty to increase racial and socioeconomic integration in schools; grounding reform in the community through the voices of educators, parents, students, and community stakeholders because "reform is most effective when it is informed by people with real experiences and expertise with public schools and the education system" (p. 8)

In summarizing the goals of the campaign, Noguera (2011b) insists that past school reform efforts to help students in poverty failed because reformers pursued a "school-alone" approach, instead of adopting "an ecological framework . . . to achieve sustainable progress in public education" (p. 13).

Wraparound initiatives. Ravitch (2014) recommends inter-related "wraparound" solutions to help equalize the playing field for students in poverty. Solutions include maintaining a health clinic with a nurse or doctor in each school, afterschool and summer programs that go beyond academics by offering enrichment activities in the arts and sports (e.g., swimming lessons, tennis lessons, science camps, museum visits, chess clubs), and parent education. Ravitch highlights successful "nurse-family partnerships" where nurses in 40 states work with poor women during pregnancy and for two years afterward to help with dietary issues, monitoring the baby's weight, and preventing substance abuse (pp. 259–260).

Having a doctor, nurse, or clinic in every school might seem unrealistic, but it can happen in even the most underserved neighborhoods. The Benjamin Franklin Elementary School in the Bronx, for example, has an on-site hospital as a result of its partnership with the Montefiore Medical Center. The affiliation with Montefiore, initiated by the principal, Luis Torres, enables the school to serve the emotional and physical needs of its 700 students, 93 percent of whom receive free and reduced lunch (ASCD, 2015b). Stephen Ritz, a 6th grade teacher, has built a tower garden in the school as well as a soil-based garden outside that helps feed students and gives unemployed parents an opportunity to learn how to farm (Colangelo, 2015). Ritz uses gardening to increase student interest in STEM subjects in hopes that some will apply to attend the specialized Bronx High School of Science.

The ASCD Whole Child approach. Championing children is at the heart of ASCD's five "Whole Child tenets," which advocate for every child's right to enter school *healthy*, learn in a physically and emotionally *safe* environment, *engage* in active learning, have the opportunity to personalize learning *supported* by qualified and caring teachers, and be academically *challenged* to succeed in college and our global community (see www.ascd.org/wholechild). ASCD

(2015c) also offers several strategies and practices to meet the needs of underserved students, summarized below:

• **Healthy**—Because of higher rates of infections, illnesses, and nutritional issues among students in poverty, schools should provide on-site access to social workers, physicians, dentists, vision and hearing specialists, and counselors to address family and mental health issues.

• **Safe**—Absenteeism, bullying, and school climate and disciplinary issues can be tackled by initiating school policies developed with the input of students, staff, and the community.

• **Engaged**—Advisory periods, personalized learning communities, and culturally relevant curricula can help create a culture to build trust with and foster the engagement of underserved students.

• **Supported**—Schools must cultivate mentorship and internship opportunities for students, as high-poverty schools often do not have access to adult-supported networks of coaches, counselors, and health professionals who can assist with important actions (e.g., filling out college applications).

• **Challenged**—Reforms must be advanced that guarantee multiple higher-level education options such as AP classes, International Baccalaureate programs, and dual-enrollment programs. Academic and social support strategies with tutors and mentors must accompany such efforts. Unfortunately, the sorting and tracking of students often begins as early as kindergarten. When remedial and gifted programs in elementary schools separate the underserved from the privileged, it becomes extremely difficult for the former to ever catch up with the latter (Darling-Hammond, 2010). School administrators, counselors, teachers, and family advocates must vigilantly block actions that unfairly discriminate against students by way of class placement.

Public Advocacy

Public advocacy for underserved students must be organized by educational practitioners, parents, community members, and other informed stakeholders to affect legislation. Many professional educational associations (e.g., AERA, ASCD, NAESP, NASSP, NEA, PDK) actively lobby state and federal lawmakers, and it is critical for practitioners to become part of this process. Lewis and Burd-Sharps (2016) note that overcoming educational inequity is impossible without first investing in reform efforts to address "residential segregation by race and income, poverty, the absence of meaningful work, unsafe neighborhoods, lack of voice and political power, and discrimination" (p. 12). Until reforms are enacted and successful, practitioners must continue full speed ahead with students who can ill afford to wait for societal institutions to garner the political will to do their job.

✅ Action Checklist to Avoid the Business "Solution" and Promote Championing and Empowering the Underserved

When considering reform initiatives during collaboration:

_____ 1. Examine each reform proposal to ensure the initiative does not hurt any single demographic group.

_____ 2. Advocate for innovative reforms that emphasize asset-based teaching strategies and culturally responsive instructional practices.

_____ 3. Discuss the implications of school reforms based on business practices that discount individual differences and the rights of students with special needs.

_____ 4. Consider the effects of data-driven tests that often undermine students who are living in poverty, are English language learners, or have special needs.

_____ 5. Pursue ESSA practices that allow for performance indicators beyond high-stakes tests (e.g., social-emotional learning strategies).

_____ 6. Use hybrid strategies to synthesize the best elements of business and education practices.

_____ 7. Reach out to engage families that have limited access to schools (e.g., through home visits and culturally responsive strategies).

_____ 8. Advocate for initiatives that involve school-community partnerships and champion full-service schools (e.g., the Comer Process, the Harlem Children's Zone).

_____ 9. Support initiatives that promote antibullying strategies and protect all vulnerable groups. Every student has the right to attend a safe school.

_____ 10. Consider reforms that align with the ASCD Whole Child approach, recognizing that a student's success in school and as a global citizen involves addressing a child's academic, health, and safety needs in a comforting environment that underscores each child's unique talents.

Chapter Reflections: Questions and Activities

Please feel free to adapt these questions and activities to meet individual or interactive group goals.

Questions

1. Place yourself in the position of a business executive or valued employee of a company selling a particular product or service. How does that role compare and contrast to a school administrator or teacher? Consider everyday responsibilities, organizational goals, and how you would define success. Share your conclusions on the different roles.

2. What are some of the advantages and disadvantages for educators seeking strategies and solutions from disciplines beyond education?

3. What are the risks for educators who become insular when tackling educational challenges? Are there benefits?

4. What teaching and learning strategies should teachers incorporate to move from a deficit-based approach to an asset-based approach? Review the ideas of Jackson and McDermott presented on pages 153–154 before addressing this question.

5. How should educators respond to stakeholders who suggest that poverty is just an excuse for teachers and administrators who are failing to make a difference with students?

6. What recommendations and strategies in this chapter resonated with you? What would you add?

7. Based on reading this chapter, what new insights, ahas, or concerns do you have?

8. What beliefs has this chapter reaffirmed?

9. What additional questions need to be asked?

Interactive Activity: Sharing "Big Ideas" from Inside and Outside Education

1. Create groups of three to four members. Each group member reflects on and writes about two "Big Ideas" (e.g., concepts, principles, movements) that have significantly affected his or her thinking about educational reform. One idea should be from the education field, and the other, from a different field or area outside of education (e.g., the business world, the world of medicine, a personal encounter, a travel experience). Consider ideas that were aha moments for you or that changed your thinking or behavior.

2. Group members share their Big Ideas, explaining how and why they were affected by them.

3. When everyone has shared, members discuss one another's ideas and consider ways to synthesize or tinker with them. Members then choose two Big Ideas other than their own that resonate with them and explain how they might affect their practice, their approach to reform, or any actions outside of education.

4. All the groups share out highlights of their conversations.

5. Discuss any takeaways.

Conclusions: A Dialogue Among 3 Teachers and 10 Takeaways to Support Reforms of Substance

As long as people talk and listen to one
another, everything remains possible.

Elie Wiesel

Principle #14: When a diverse group of individuals engage in thoughtful collaboration, and know that what they say and do is valued, then actions to improve schools can become a moral enterprise.

There are no perfect formulas to guarantee the success of a reform initiative. And unfortunately, a crystal ball will not help. But educators are optimists; after all, we work with incredible colleagues and students. We take pride in knowing that the high school graduation rate has reached a national record, 83.2 percent (IES, 2016), but are also the first to lament: What about the other 16.8 percent? And what about the disparities between affluent and underserved students? We know we can do better. That is why I wrote this book: to help educators and other stakeholders do a better job of promoting reforms of substance and reducing the effects of harmful fads.

A Dialogue Among 3 Teachers

The six red flags and six guidelines examined in the previous chapters are interrelated concepts. The following scenario provides a succinct summary of the concepts and demonstrates, in a practical and lighthearted way, *how* they are interrelated. The play is a dialogue among three teachers in Mr. McMurren's classroom, with the principal, Ms. Liu, joining at the very end. As you read it, try to identify all 12 red flags and guidelines. (You can use the checklist in Figure 8 to check off each concept as you identify it.)

FIGURE 8
Checklist of Red Flags and Guidelines

Red Flags	Guidelines
___The Narrative Trap	___Building a Collaborative Learning Community
___Overpromising and Overloading	___Effectively Using Human, Fiscal, and Material Resources
___Minimizing the Enormous Difficulty of Implementation	___Respecting the Change Process
___Eyes Off the Prize	___Sustaining a Coherent School Mission and Vision
___Historical Amnesia	___Embracing Timeless and Eclectic Teaching Practices
___The Business "Solution"	___Championing and Empowering the Underserved

Mr. Frank McMurren's Social Studies Classroom 203:

Where Red Flags Meet Their Match

A Play in One Act

Cast of Characters

Frank McMurren   A veteran social studies teacher with 20 years of experience

Charles Freemont   A new English teacher

Mary Lambert   A veteran math teacher with 25 years of experience

Mei Liu   The high school principal

Scene

Mr. McMurren's Classroom

Time

It is the Wednesday before Labor Day, six days before school begins at Frederick Douglass High School. It is 8:00 a.m. A faculty meeting begins in one hour.

FRANK

(In the room alone, thinking to himself)

I already feel rushed, and we have our first faculty meeting in about an hour. I'm really nervous about next Tuesday. You would think that after 20 years of teaching the butterflies would finally disappear. My reputation with the students, the administration, and parents is good, but it feels like my first year all over again. Maybe it's because I had to change classrooms. I just wish they hadn't painted this summer and moved all of my stuff. I can't find anything! The new teachers must really be feeling it.

(Knock on the door)

FRANK

Come in!

CHARLES
(Walking over to Mr. McMurren and shaking his hand)

Mr. McMurren, hi! It's me, Charles Freemont. We met last March when I was student-teaching in Ms. Jane Greenwald's English class. Thanks for agreeing to mentor me this year. It was good observing you in the spring, I learned a lot.

FRANK
*(Realizing he hadn't thought about Charles
for one moment during the summer)*

Charles! Oh, um . . . yeah. How are you? I forgot we were going to be working together this year, but, hey—great! We'll make it work! We'll learn from each other. I'm not that familiar with all the new ideas at the university, and Jane mentioned in the spring that you were really good with technology. She said you helped her with blended learning—maybe you can help me too.

Oh, sorry, please sit down. And call me Frank.

CHARLES
(Grabbing a chair and sitting down next to Frank)

Thanks, uh, Frank. I've been working hard all summer to prepare for my classes. I'm teaching three sections of English 9 and one class of juniors. Ms. Liu said since I have one open period I'll be teaching an elective class. I thought with all your experience, you could help me choose the elective. I have to tell Ms. Liu by tomorrow; she gave me a few choices. She heard from Ms. Greenwald that I was good in technology. Ms. Liu wants to know if I can teach the class Coding for Careers or this new elective they have called The Maker Movement. I hear the school bought a new, $4,000 3-D printer for that maker movement class, with all the parts and resources you need. It'll be fun to use—I can learn along with the students! There is also an elective, only for juniors and seniors, on Shakespeare. I wonder why another teacher hasn't been assigned to that class? I'm not really an expert on Shakespeare, so I don't think I should teach the course. I would never tell my students, but I didn't really like studying Shakespeare. I don't think it's relevant for today. I don't know, maybe I shouldn't say that. Hey, Mr. McMurren—I mean, Frank—what do you think I should do? Which elective should I teach? Oh, I'm also going to be the assistant coach of the debate team this year, working with Ms. Greenwald.

FRANK

Charles, I hope you don't mind me saying this but, just listening to you, maybe taking on the Shakespeare class would be a good thing. When you say Shakespeare's not relevant . . . I feel funny telling you this, since you're the English teacher, but it sounds like you aren't open to hearing how Shakespeare applies to us today. You're kind of stuck in the narrative that he's not relevant, but think of the themes in his plays! Ambition, jealousy, treason, betrayal—they're *all* still relevant today. I once heard a friend say that if you want to study human behavior, you're better off studying Shakespeare than Freud.

Sorry, I should apologize. I don't really want to tell you what to do.

CHARLES

Don't apologize, I asked for your advice. Actually, you make a good point. The truth is, I got a *C* in Shakespeare in college. Part of the reason I tune out Shakespeare is that I had a bad experience with the course. The professor didn't really like me. I know there's a Shakespeare club affiliated with the bookstores in town; maybe if I collaborate with folks who love Shakespeare, I'll change my mind. Hearing a fresh point of view might help. Please don't tell Ms. Greenwald or Ms. Liu about my Shakespeare problem. Let me think about teaching the class. Mmm, but I need to make a decision by tomorrow. I hope my Shakespeare college professor isn't in the book club! *(Laughing nervously)*

FRANK

I heard about purchasing that 3-D printer. Wow, 4,000 bucks. I don't know, sounds crazy.

(Knock on the door. Mary Lambert, a good teaching friend of Frank's, enters, grabs a chair, and sits down next to Charles.)

MARY

Frank, it was great getting together Sunday with the families. Thanks for the barbeque. We had a fun time. Can't believe how big your kids have gotten! Charles, I remember you from last year. Jane Greenwald said you were one of her hardest-working student teachers.

CHARLES

Thanks, I'm looking forward to this year, and I know I'm lucky to have Mr. McMurren—um, Frank—as my mentor.

FRANK

Mary, did you hear about this new 3-D printer the school bought? I mean, 4,000 bucks! What were they thinking?

MARY

Frank . . . look, I was on the STEM team that made the decision to buy it. Believe me, we did our homework! I personally checked with three districts that had gone through the experience. One district bought a printer five years ago, and to be honest with you, I don't think they knew what they were doing. Their principal attended a seminar on technology and came back to the school all excited about 3-D printers. I heard the printer just sat there for a year. The other two districts have been actively using the printers. One school has a strong STEM program with a couple of architects from the community joining the students every couple of weeks. They've created prototype miniature cars and robotic devices, and they are working on renewable energy tools. All activities are aligned with the science or math curriculum. They did their homework.

And Frank, we did ours. Our STEM team is working with Lindsey, the district IT director. We have a three-year funding plan built into the budget. We are going to use the printer in our math program, and the science teachers are going to use it, too. Lindsey will join our department meetings this year and share the training she received on integrating the printer into our programs. But we are going to go slow. It still makes me sick when I think about those PalmPilots we bought for the faculty about 15 years ago as a time management tool that no one ended up using. No training, nothing. At the time, we thought they were the greatest. Who was on that committee again? *(Frank blushes.)* Those devices are still in the stockroom, you know.

CHARLES

Wow, I didn't realize so much work goes into buying stuff for the school. I was thinking about teaching the maker movement elective and learning how to use the 3-D printer with the students, but I don't know. I mentioned it to a couple of friends last night about whether to take the maker movement class or coding class. They were excited for me and encouraged me to go with coding. "It will be easy," they said. "You'll just build stuff. Or learn how to code from the students. It's just a one-semester elective." I don't know, I haven't thought about a curriculum or goals. I was just thinking we would just, you know, do it and learn along the way.

I think I'll tell Ms. Liu this afternoon that we can cross those two courses off the list. By the way, what are PalmPilots?

MARY

(Laughing)

PalmPilots were among the first PDAs, but before we knew it smartphones appeared, and they became obsolete. They were a flash in the pan. The newest shiny object! We thought they were going to meet the time management needs of every teacher—a magic bullet. The PalmPilots were supposed to be really easy to implement. Folks thought they were going to transform how we manage our time and organize our lessons. The brochure said something like, "Reduce your planning time by 50 percent!" Every student was going to benefit because we would have student information at our fingertips. I remember the software glitches, and there was no training. Frank, didn't the district buy one for everybody? *(Frank shrugs his shoulders.)* Anyway, Charles, if you want to see what they look like, go to the stockroom. I think they're next to the old student handbooks from 1999.

CHARLES

Because I have both of you here, let me ask you about something else. I know you're both good friends with Ms. Greenwald. She probably told you about her plans to retire next year. Said I might be the next head debate coach. Well, Ms. Greenwald told me she spends a lot of time, about a week, reviewing Socratic questioning strategies and going over strategies from the Lincoln-Douglas debates. I'm not sure that's worth the time, especially because we already have the list of policy debate topics for this year's state competition. Should I say something? I think we should start researching information about the new debate topics. I was on the debate team in my high school, and we always did really well because we were the most prepared. Facts make a difference. Also, there is some great software for curating information for this year's policy topics. I could show everyone on the team how to use it.

(Mary and Frank briefly glance at each other.)

FRANK

Charles, am I right that when you started student-teaching, the debate competition was just about over? *(Charles nods.)* So you're not really sure how the program worked here? *(Charles nods again, guiltily this time.)* Charles, I know you probably learned some great strategies from your high school coach, and that facts are important, but everyone runs their program a little differently.

MARY

Also, Jane has won a lot of competitions over the years. I've seen her teach. She believes in time-tested strategies. There's a reason that strategies from Socrates and the Lincoln-Douglas debates are still used in classrooms today. One reason Jane is such a good teacher is that she has a talent for choosing content. You don't know this, but 20 years ago she was the major force behind changing a lot of the books on the state English adoption list. Contemporary women, Hispanic, black, and Asian authors were hard to find on the state list before Jane got involved. It wasn't just about changing the content for her. I still remember her speaking with the faculty about process. Jane wanted to change the list to inspire more students to get involved in English classes, especially students from underrepresented groups. I mean, how could Maya Angelou be left out of the high school curriculum? Her work isn't just great literature, it teaches students about civil rights, racism, and the treatment of women. But Jane is also firm about keeping the past in focus. She still enjoys teaching *Moby-Dick,* and if you ask her, she loves teaching *Romeo and Juliet. (Frank and Charles both laugh.)* What's so funny?

CHARLES

Let's just say I'm learning to love Shakespeare today.

MARY

Charles, just one other thought about Jane's approach and what you can bring to the table. Teaching doesn't have to be an either/or choice between ideas and process. I think the debate team will be great this year, with Jane's emphasis on process and what you will bring to enrich the content.

FRANK

Basically, what we're saying is, teaching isn't just about facts. Hey, I teach history—I love facts, but facts alone are a big yawn with students; history needs to be about stories. Use this year to observe how Jane coaches the debate team. But definitely suggest using the software you mentioned, too. What did you say it did? Curate information on this year's debate topics? I agree with Mary, the two of you will make a great team! The fact that she asked you to be the assistant coach tells me a lot. The debate team is her baby. I wasn't a teacher at Douglass when Jane started, but I was told that before she took it over, no one was interested in debate.

MARY

What is most impressive is that some of the students on the debate team were like diamonds in the rough. Other teachers, myself included, sometimes don't notice how talented our students are. Jane can spot talent. Because of her, our expectations for her debate students completely changed. I know that in my math classes, when I have debate students who have been successful at district and state competitions, I push them harder, because they have already demonstrated their grit and perseverance. It just reminds me how important it is to have high expectations for all students.

CHARLES

I can't tell you how much I appreciate everything you've been telling me. It's actually blowing me away. I know our faculty meeting starts in a few minutes. One other thing, I got to work really early this morning because I wanted to access the web-based school management system to have it in place for Tuesday, but it seems to be down. I called the district IT office but just got a recording about three workshops before Tuesday that everyone is invited to. I really want to go over the data on my students to get to know them. If I can learn how they scored on the state tests the last few years, I'll have a good picture of what they are capable of. By the way, last spring, when Ms. Greenwald showed me how to work the old management system, I felt like I was snooping on the students a little. I'm only, like, five years older than some of them. And this is a little funny, but one of the national debate topics this year is whether the U.S. government should be curtailing its surveillance of its citizens. Anyway, when the management system is working, how much do you use the data?

MARY

(Smiling)

Charles, I'm going to tell you a little secret. Although the faculty manual says we should review the statistical data carefully so we have the data on each student at our fingertips, well . . . each teacher handles it differently. Some of us ignore the data altogether, because we don't want to prejudge how the students will do in our classes. Some of our most capable students simply don't test well. Personally, I think the tests are biased. How can students who have been in the country for less than a year and know very little English possibly do well on the state ELA test? If you want to know how much these students know, test them in the three languages they already speak!

FRANK

Charles, as Mary knows, I look at the family information. What are their last names? Do their parents or guardians have separate addresses? The district office is supposed to let us know which students are homeless, which is really helpful. I probably use the statistical data more than Mary. She has it all in her head anyway—*(smiling at Mary)* before the end of the year she'll make sure you know she is a math genius! But she's right, be careful with data. It's not just about numbers. Find out each student's story. It's actually amazing how well some of our students do when you find out about their home responsibilities and personal stories. Some hold two jobs while helping their mothers take care of three brothers and grandma. Charles, you have to advocate for these students. Sometimes they get a raw deal in school, too. When you make decisions about class assignments, ask yourself: Will this decision hurt any of my students?

MARY

You're right, Frank, I am a math genius. The only thing I would add is that every student in our school needs an advocate. When I hear administrators talk about school reform, it's always about programs for students who are underserved or about how we have to do better with our most talented students, whatever that means. Let's not forget the students who are in the middle—the ones who aren't great students but also aren't in dire straits. They need advocates, too.

I guess I feel this way because no one noticed me in high school. I wasn't really motivated but could always get by. I would see teachers say hi to other students in the hallway and just walk right past me. It hurt. We need to catch *all* our students. I always check out our school mission statement at the beginning of the year. I know I may be the only one *(Mary and Frank laugh)*, but honestly, I find it inspirational. *(Mary walks over to the wall near the classroom door where a copy of the school mission is posted.)* "The Frederick Douglass School believes in possibility. We celebrate the opportunity, and embrace the responsibility, to provide each student with an exceptional Douglass experience where they can excel academically, pursue nonacademic interests and passions to reach college and career goals, and live fulfilling lives as citizens of the nation and the global community." As Frank always says, words matter. Charles, keep the mission in mind.

(Knock on the door. The principal, Mei Liu, sticks her head in, looking at her watch.)

FRANK AND MARY

Hey, Mei.

CHARLES

Good morning, Ms. Liu.

MEI

Good morning. Great to see everyone! Frank, it killed me not to go to your barbeque on Sunday, but I was buried here all day. Thanks for the invite! Sorry to bother everyone, but the e-mail is down, we are scrambling to get the new web-based school management software ready, and there are software glitches everywhere in the district. I just want to remind you all of the faculty meeting. Oh, glad to see Charles here, with the two of you. Charles, Mary and Frank are the best! Pay attention to what they have to say, even though nobody else does. The meeting is in five minutes. By the way, Frank, didn't you promise me you would take the PalmPilots to the recycling center this summer? After about two decades that will be your last act as head of the Innovations Committee from way back in the day! *(Mei laughs as she closes the door. Mary gives Frank a strange look.)*

THE END

Were you able to spot the six red flags and six guidelines? If you have an opportunity to do so, talk with a colleague and compare notes. Don't be surprised if you disagree a little—Mary, Frank, Charles, and Mei sometimes felt a need to make more than one point each time they spoke!

10 Takeaways to Support Reforms of Substance

Principle #15: Implementing reforms begins with building relationships.

The following 10 takeaways offer a reflective overview of crucial points examined in this book. Some of the takeaways are syntheses of several key ideas. Consider these points as additional guidelines for pursuing reforms of substance. After reading, think about what you would add to the list.

1. Educators should break away from personal and professional narratives. We are each captive to our personal history, narrative, and worldview. This isn't totally unhealthy—we should take pride in our history and beliefs. But if our personal narratives make it impossible to listen to or understand the world beyond our doorstep, that's a problem. Recall the discussion of *confirmation bias* in Chapter 2 (see pp. 28–29) when individuals "ignore evidence that contradicts their preconceived notions" (Kahneman et al., 2011, p. 51). Contrary views liberate us by providing us with more information to make better decisions.

2. The central role of context in the school improvement process requires humility. As Russakoff put it, "Education reform is too important to be left to reformers alone" (2015a, p. 213). The work of school reform is humbling everyone, because context makes every situation different. There will always be setbacks. The goal of the Newark reformers (see Chapter 2, pp. 47–48) was to make the district a national "proof point" of success and then replicate the strategies in other urban school districts. It was a noble goal, if a naive one.

More humility on the part of the reformers would have helped. The *failure to frequently seek feedback from the community* about their schools and the community was a critical error. As Zenger and Folkman note, "Humility will make you approachable" (2002, p. 236).

3. Leadership is key to retaining teachers. When teachers can be counted on to work in the same school for several years, student performance improves (Johnson, 2012). Educators, policymakers, and reformers who want to positively reform schools should target teacher retention as central to their work. Effective school leadership is a major aspect of that equation. According to Johnson, high teacher turnover rates are less the result of student issues than a response to organizational characteristics—particularly a lack of supportive leadership and a weak culture of collaboration (p. 115). One of the most important roles of a school principal is to help shape a supportive and trusting school environment. It takes years to be an effective teacher, and good principals support seasoned educators by building relationships, providing feedback, and letting the teachers know that their good work is never taken for granted.

4. Teaching is complex. How the notion that teaching is easy ever gained traction is hard to understand. If reformers are serious about gaining the trust and credibility of teachers, they should keep their distance from this unwise notion. One reason the profession is so challenging is that just when teachers think they have it figured out—say, four or five years into the job—a challenging student or class comes along that takes them back to the drawing board. Each day brings surprises, and daily feedback from students keeps teachers on their toes. Fine-tuning instruction should be every teacher's daily ritual.

5. Educators must support underserved students. Students often suffer due to adverse circumstances for which they bear no responsibility. Educators must always ask, Will the reforms we are considering hurt any particular group of students? Fortunately, through initiatives like the Comer Process, students and parents are gaining decision-making power. Teachers and principals need to work on two fronts: in school, to ensure that all students have equal access to quality teaching and resources, and outside of school, to advocate for social safety net resources and social justice and begin leveling the playing field. In school, teachers and administrators can make a considerable contribution when they provide both social support *and* a rigorous, comprehensive academic program. All children and youth need to believe in their future. Payne's (2008) advice for teachers and administrators is a good place to start: "Above all, no matter where in the social structure children are coming from, act as if their possibilities are boundless. I don't know that all of our research and work and experimentation have given us any more clarity than that" (p. 212).

6. Educators must support technology initiatives using timeless and eclectic strategies. Remember the mantra: *Pedagogy precedes technology*. The success of San Francisco's Exploratorium (see Chapter 6, pp. 126–127) demonstrates that when scientists and museum directors study pedagogy and embrace their teaching lineage, students benefit greatly.

7. If it doesn't have a positive effect on teaching and learning, then it's not reform. The central question to ask when a new initiative is proposed is, How will this affect the classroom, student progress, and the interaction between students and teachers? I once had a graduate student mention that what impressed the public most was how quickly schools repaired building damages or fixed hazards on the playground. By contrast, he said, the actual work of students in classrooms, or of teacher professional development, rarely interested the public. But of course, structural reforms (i.e., visual changes) have little to do with teaching and learning.

8. Collaboration and social capital are essential. There is no better feeling than being part of a school where everyone is committed to student success and believes in a collective mission to carry out the sacred work of teaching and learning. Building social capital is part of that work because it binds the school and community through mutual earned trust, collaborative relationship building, and pride in the ongoing success of students (Leanna, 2011). Additionally, when an organization is healthy and social capital is strong, teachers, staff, administrators, and community members are better equipped to cope when the setbacks occur.

9. Educators must remain faithful to the mission and vision. The school or district vision enables educators to imagine what outstanding student work looks like in classrooms. The work may not be occurring to our satisfaction today, but visioning is about closing the gap between a present reality and potential. The mission anchors the vision by clarifying the purpose of schooling. The mission answers the question, Why do we exist?

10. Schools are like barn-raising communities. The beauty of a barn raising is that everyone plays a role. The community takes pride in bringing people and resources together to accomplish a worthy goal. Community members plan thoughtfully to acquire resources and tap a diversity of skills. Unless everyone is ready to roll up their sleeves and do the hard work, nothing gets done. No one is watching passively from the balcony; everyone is on the stage. If a few experts think that they can come in with "superior" knowledge and skills to direct the project—well, the barn won't get built. A barn raising works because the individuals working the knobs and nails are just as respected as those designing the frame or selecting the setting.

All of us can learn from those who use their hands, heads, and hearts to collaborate harmoniously. It takes a tight-knit collaborative community willing to embrace the guidelines in this book to make a real difference for students and teachers.

Now, let's go build that barn!

Appendix A: Protocols for Discussions on Red Flags and Guidelines

Protocols are tools educators can use for guiding *a structured collaborative discussion to unpack thinking on important ideas.* Facilitators play an important role in the process, keeping the conversation focused and ensuring that the discussion is conducted in a respectful manner. Depending on the relationships among discussion participants, it may be necessary for facilitators to conduct icebreakers to assist with introductions and group norms to build trust and respect.

The two protocols presented here address the red flags and guidelines discussed throughout this book. Each session should take 60 to 90 minutes depending on the size of the group (90 to 120 minutes if using both protocols in a single session). The facilitator and group participants should feel free not to discuss the chapters in order—it's fine to start with Chapter 3, for instance, before moving on to Chapter 2.

If a session examines an entire chapter (that is, both the red flag and the guideline sections), the facilitator should review the two protocols and merge some questions to meet group objectives and time constraints. The protocol format is based on experiences with my graduate classes, workshops, and excellent protocol resources

(Easton, 2009; Gawande, 2010; McDonald, Mohr, Dichter, & McDonald, 2013; Walsh & Sattes, 2015).

Protocol 1: Red Flags

Purpose: This protocol provides recommendations and steps to organize and engage in an in-depth collaborative discussion of each red flag discussed in Chapters 2–7: the narrative trap, overpromising and overloading, minimizing the enormous difficulty of implementation, eyes off the prize, historical amnesia, and the business "solution." Each session is devoted to analyzing one red flag.

Goals: To examine how red flags inhibit districts, schools, and individual teachers from pursuing reforms of substance

Norms: Respecting the contributions of each participant, applauding listening skills, opposing disparaging or "blaming" remarks, limiting digressions, and establishing the benefits of community; the facilitator should acknowledge the wealth of knowledge present and the importance of each individual encouraging others to participate in the discussion

Participants: Any stakeholders in a school reform effort are welcome to participate.

Time Frame: 60 to 90 minutes if only the red flag section is discussed, 90 to 120 minutes for the whole chapter

Preparation: Facilitators and participants will read the selected red flag section prior to convening, and facilitators make note of five quotes to share with participants in Step A. Depending on the size of the group, consider breaking it up into smaller groups (job-alike, self-selected, cross-grade or department representatives in each group, or more diverse setups if a wide range of stakeholders are involved). Small groups should periodically share information with the larger group.

Steps:

A. Icebreaker: Participants spend five minutes reading the quotes preselected by the facilitator, select the one that resonates with them the most, and discuss their selections with a partner. Time permitting, participants can also choose a quote of their own to share and discuss.

B. Overview: The facilitator briefly describes each subsection of the red flag section under discussion and shares one or two essential ideas or themes from selected subsections that tie the greater whole together.

C. Questions: Participants discuss the following questions as a whole group or in smaller groups:

1. What is it about the red flag that inhibits the ability of educators to pursue reforms of substance and inadvertently contributes to the possible implementation of fads?

2. What are two to four essential ideas from the red flag section? What dilemmas do these ideas present? (Participants take two or three minutes to write a few notes before sharing, skimming through the chapter text if necessary.)

3. Which ideas related to the red flag were particularly discomforting, puzzling (causing you to pause and review the idea), concerning, or surprising? What truths has this red flag section affirmed for you? (This is a good opportunity for Pair-Share.)

4. How does this red flag *contextually* relate to your district, school, or classroom? Can any ideas be applied now? Is this red flag a barrier to change efforts in your district, school, or classroom?

5. How can this red flag section contribute to decision making and other actions in your district, school, or classroom?

6. Why is it difficult to avoid this red flag? How does it contribute to promoting educational fads?

7. On a scale of 1 to 5, how much is this red flag an obstacle to pursuing reforms of substance? (1 = not an obstacle; 5 = a major obstacle)

D. Reflections: Participants take two to three minutes to write down two or three new insights or concerns *that the discussion raised* and share with one another. The facilitator asks participants if they have any additional questions.

E. Debriefing: The facilitator asks participants: What are your thoughts on the effectiveness of the protocol process? Participants share ideas for fine-tuning the protocol for future sessions.

Protocol 2: Guidelines

Purpose: This protocol provides recommendations and steps to organize and engage in an in-depth collaborative discussion of each guideline discussed in Chapters 2–7: building a collaborative community; effectively using human, fiscal, and material resources; respecting the change process; sustaining a coherent school mission and vision; embracing timeless and eclectic teaching practices; and championing and empowering the underserved. Each protocol session is devoted to analyzing one guideline.

Goals: To examine and highlight guidelines that can help promote and sustain initiatives that improve teaching and learning while disrupting the effects of red flags

Norms: Refer to the red flag protocol section.

Participants: Any stakeholders in a school reform effort are welcome to participate.

Time Frame: 60 to 90 minutes if only the guideline section is discussed, 90 to 120 minutes for the whole chapter

Preparation: Facilitators and participants will read the selected guideline section prior to convening, and facilitators make note of five quotes to share with participants in Step A. Depending on the size of the group, consider breaking it up into smaller groups (job-alike, self-selected, cross-grade or department representatives in each group, or more diverse setups if a wide range of stakeholders are involved). Small groups should periodically share information with the larger group.

Steps:

A. Icebreaker Emphasizing Practical Recommendations: Participants spend five minutes reading the quotes preselected by the facilitator, select the one that resonates with them the most, and discuss their selections with a partner. Time permitting, participants can also choose a quote of their own.

B. Overview: The facilitator briefly describes each subsection of the guideline section under discussion and shares one or two essential ideas or themes from selected subsections that tie the greater whole together.

C. Questions: Participants discuss the following questions as a whole group or in smaller groups:

1. How does this guideline section support important reforms? How can the guideline reduce the effects of the red flag noted in this chapter or other red flags?

2. What are two to four essential ideas from the guideline section? Although the ideas may be useful in your situation, what dilemmas do these ideas present? (Participants take two or three minutes to write a few notes before sharing, skimming through the chapter text if necessary.)

3. Which strategies, recommendations, or essential ideas are you already using from this guideline section? What additional practices are you using that were not mentioned in the section? What ideas related to the guideline are discomforting (causing you to pause and review the idea), concerning, or surprising? What truths has this guideline section affirmed for you? (This is a good opportunity for Pair-Share.)

4. How does this guideline *contextually* relate to your district, school, or classroom? Can any ideas be applied now? Is this guideline a barrier to change efforts in your district, school, or classroom?

5. How can the guideline, recommendations, practices, and essential ideas in this section contribute to decision making and other actions in your district, school, or classroom?

6. In small groups, create a brainstorming list of three to five practical guidelines and recommendations related to the chapter section. With the facilitator's help, try to reach a consensus of three to five guidelines from the whole group.

7. Group members should share their best advice, strategies, and recommendations from personal experiences, and from books and articles, related to the chapter section.

D. & E. Reflections and Debriefing: Refer to the red flag protocol section.

Appendix B: Questions to Promote Collaborative Discussions of Red Flags and Guidelines

Purpose: These questions will help schools and districts engage in collaborative discussions when considering new initiatives. Discussions will help stakeholders recognize and disrupt harmful fads while supporting reforms of substance to affect teaching and learning.

A Note About Context: The *context* of each district, school, and classroom is different. Local decision makers should consider these differences when answering questions.

Directions: For each question below, write any comments in the column on the right and discuss with colleagues. Consider: Is the school or district comfortable making an immediate decision about an initiative under consideration?

Red Flags

Red Flag	Definition	Questions	Comments
The Narrative Trap	Isolation created by ignoring narratives, opinions, data, and feedback contrary to our narrative and beliefs	___ 1. Do educators in the school or district represent a variety of different instructional approaches? ___ 2. Do most educators in the school or district have an open mind about contrary ideas? ___ 3. Are particular narratives about the initiative dominant in the school or district? Is that good or bad? ___ 4. Does the school or district culture welcome educational ideas contrary to the initiative under consideration? ___ 5. Are educators in the school or district committed to previous decisions that relate to the initiative? ___ 6. Are educators in the school or district satisfied that the initiative is the best option for students based on merit and research? ___ 7. Are educators in the school or district willing to proactively examine research about the initiative contrary to their beliefs? ___ 8. Have alternative initiatives been considered? ___ 9. Have the interests and values of the community been taken into account when considering the initiative?	

Red Flag	Definition	Questions	Comments
Overpromising and Overloading	Overpromising: unrealistic and sometimes harmful guarantees of reform success Overloading: tackling too many initiatives simultaneously	___ 1. How many major initiatives are presently being supported in the school or district? ___ 2. Will the initiative under consideration modify or eliminate another program? ___ 3. If the initiative is adopted, is there a risk of overloading teachers or overloading students? ___ 4. What other major initiatives are on the horizon? ___ 5. Have staff in the school or district been inclined toward instructional "quick fixes"? Does this affect the initiative under consideration? ___ 6. Has the initiative been marketed to staff in the school or district as addressing the needs of *all* students? Does it have the potential to do so? ___ 7. If the initiative involves new technology, does the school or district have the infrastructure to support the initiative?	
Minimizing the Enormous Difficulty of Implementation	Innocently neglecting or arrogantly discounting the complexity and difficulty of implementing substantive school change initiatives	___ 1. What roadblocks to implementation need to be considered and addressed about this particular initiative? Are there unique issues related to the initiative (e.g., it's experimental or a pilot study)? ___ 2. Have contextual issues been carefully weighed with respect to students, teachers, leadership, instructional resources, professional development, finances, the length of the commitment, and community buy-in? ___ 3. If the reform involves new practices, what professional development strategies are planned? ___ 4. Has the initiative been marketed as "easy to implement" or "no teacher training necessary"? ___ 5. Is the school or district piloting the initiative? If not, why not? ___ 6. What stakeholder groups in and out of the school need to be involved with implementing the initiative? Is the community involved in the process?	

Red Flag	Definition	Questions	Comments
Eyes Off the Prize	When primary goals are undermined by secondary interests	___ 1. Will this initiative help accomplish a primary goal related to students, or is it being driven by a secondary interest? What can be done to ensure that addressing student needs is the primary goal? How will students benefit from the initiative? ___ 2. Are educators embracing the initiative for fear of being left behind or to "keep up with the Joneses"? ___ 3. If the initiative involves technology, are student needs driving the process? What are the plans for professional development? ___ 4. Who are the main sponsors of the initiative (e.g., local or state educators, parents, policymakers, vendors, for-profit corporations, researchers, foundation professionals, community activists)? ___ 5. Does the sponsor understand the contextual needs of the school or district? ___ 6. Is research available supporting the initiative independent of the sponsor?	
Historical Amnesia	Making little or no effort to explore the historical antecedents of a proposed initiative	___ 1. Is the initiative new or an iteration of an earlier one? ___ 2. Have educators reviewed the local and national lineage of the initiative? If yes, what have they learned? ___ 3. Is the initiative a reaction to a present school program? ___ 4. Have students or teachers been affected in the past by initiatives similar to the one under consideration? If yes, what has been learned? ___ 5. If the initiative is marketed as "a first" or especially innovative, what questions need to be asked? Have the sponsors provided sound, independent research with a historical perspective to support the initiative?	

Red Flag	Definition	Questions	Comments
The Business "Solution"	Strategies based on Scientific Management principles—bureaucratic and data-driven group efficiency, students as merchandise, and schools as closed systems to be managed without addressing outside social, political, safety, and economic issues related to the community	___1. Does the initiative have the potential to hurt a specific student population? ___2. Will a program lose funds as a result of the initiative? ___3. Is a program going to be replaced as a result of the initiative? If so, how will students be affected by eliminating the program? ___4. Can whole child considerations be integrated with the initiative (e.g., social-emotional learning goals)? ___5. Will the success of this reform be based solely on quantitative data-driven student information? How will individual growth be assessed? ___6. Was the initiative selected solely based on business principles? If so, do the principles make sense for a school? Can the principles be modified for individual students?	

Guidelines

Guideline	Definition	Questions	Comments
Building a Collaborative Learning Community	Respectfully working together as trusting and mutually accountable adults in the school and community focused on common teaching and learning goals to support reforms	___ 1. What are the most pressing needs of students in the school or district? How will the initiative contribute to those needs? ___ 2. Is social capital strong enough that educators trust each other to overcome the hurdles related to implementation? ___ 3. How can a professional learning community (PLC) play a role in sustaining the practice? What should its goals be? How will staff work together? How will they be held mutually accountable to ensure the success of the initiative? What expectations do educators have for student outcomes? Will the PLC create the professional development program for the initiative? ___ 4. Does the school or district have room for the "solo artist" who prefers not to actively collaborate on initiatives? If the solo artist successfully initiates the reform without engaging colleagues, is that good enough? ___ 5. How are staff affirming skeptics of the proposed initiative? Are staff listening to the concerns? ___ 6. How are staff involving the parent and greater community with the initiative? How are we involving families that do not have easy access to the school?	

Guideline	Definition	Questions	Comments
Effectively Using Human, Fiscal, and Material Resources	Intentionally procuring and using resources to meet the school mission, keeping excellence, equality, and equity in mind	___ 1. What is the school or district's plan to implement the initiative holistically as it relates to curriculum, instruction, assessment, and teacher professional development? Is the school or district mobilizing the resources necessary to support the initiative? ___ 2. What is the timeline for successfully implementing and institutionalizing the initiative? Does the school or district have the funds to support the timeline? ___ 3. How are we going to evaluate whether the initiative is successfully affecting instruction? ___ 4. Are plans in place in case the initiative falters due to changing circumstances? ___ 5. If the initiative depends on technology, does the budget account for this? ___ 6. Do staff have a long-term commitment from faculty and administration to support the initiative?	
Respecting the Change Process	Valuing process, patience, context, and substance; recognizing that change is meaningful when it most affects teaching and learning	___ 1. Are staff continually asking how the initiative will improve student learning? ___ 2. How are staff helping each other remember that change is a process and that positive feelings about the reform will ebb and flow? ___ 3. How can teachers be empowered to make decisions about implementation? ___ 4. Is professional development related to the reform tailored to address the needs of teachers on a continuum of skills? ___ 5. How will teachers who are having difficulties with implementation be assisted? ___ 6. Will the school or district consider the ideas of skeptics for fine-tuning the initiative?	

Guideline	Definition	Questions	Comments
Sustaining a Coherent School Mission and Vision	Making decisions about student needs based upon beliefs about how to provide an exceptional K–12 education to advance their future success	____ 1. How will the initiative help students fulfill the school mission? ____ 2. Will the initiative affect all students? How? ____ 3. Is the initiative serving a targeted population (e.g., special education, Title I)? How? ____ 4. How will the initiative be monitored to ensure that it remains aligned (i.e., coherent) with the school or district mission and vision? What is the connection between the initiative and current school policies? ____ 5. Will the initiative advance the school or district vision? If not, is that a problem? ____ 6. If the initiative deviates from the mission but is successful, should the mission be revisited?	
Embracing Timeless and Eclectic Teaching Strategies	Implementing classical and enduring teaching strategies and avoiding either/or traps that force educators to choose one good idea over another	____ 1. How will the initiative advance student needs and teacher strengths? ____ 2. Are there timeless teaching practices that are uniquely suited for integrating with the initiative (e.g., eclectic teaching, comprehensive curriculum, democratic classroom)? If so, how can their integration be ensured? ____ 3. How might the initiative strengthen other programs in the school? ____ 4. If principles and strategies related to the initiative differ from those of present school programs, how can the "Genius of the AND" approach accentuate the initiative's strengths? ____ 5. If the initiative involves technology, how can the concept of "pedagogy precedes technology" be used to help implement it successfully?	

Guideline	Definition	Questions	Comments
Championing and Empowering the Underserved	Affirming the right of each student to receive a superior education that values equity, equality, excellence, and the positive qualities that individual children bring to school; rejecting an approach to learning that discounts the effects of social and economic forces on schools	___ 1. How can we ensure that the initiative will not hurt any specific group of students? ___ 2. How will the initiative support underserved students and those living in poverty? ___ 3. How is the initiative supporting teaching strategies based on student strengths rather than deficits? ___ 4. How does the initiative align with school or district values related to excellence, equality, and equity? ___ 5. Are there aspects of the initiative that will disadvantage students living in poverty? (Will students need internet access at home?) If so, what can be done? ___ 6. How are staff reaching out to discuss the initiative with families that do not have easy access to school information (e.g., non-English-speaking communities)? ___ 7. How are we reaching out to welcome and empower nontraditional families (e.g., LGBTQ families)? ___ 8. Are there public advocacy actions that the school or district should be taking with legislators or public and private agencies?	

Appendix C: A List of Educational Initiatives, Ideas, Practices, and Trends from the Past 30-Plus Years

- Academic press and social support
- Accelerated schools
- Accountability movement
- Achievement gap
- Adequate yearly progress
- Advanced placement
- Alternative certification
- Alternative schooling
- Antibullying programs
- Assessment movement
- Asset-based approach
- Back to basics
- Balanced literacy
- Benchmarks
- Best practices
- Bilingual education
- Blended learning
- Block scheduling
- Brain-based learning
- Breaking ranks
- Budgetary reforms
- Bullying prevention
- Career technology education
- Character education
- Charter schools
- Civics education (revisited)
- Co-teaching
- Coalition of Essential Schools
- Coding
- Cognitive science and learning
- Collaboration (among students, faculty, staff, community)
- College- and career-ready standards
- Comer Process
- Common Core State Standards
- Community partnerships
- Community schools

- Competency-based education
- Consortium testing (SBAC/PARCC)
- Cooperative learning
- Core knowledge schools
- Credit recovery
- Critical friends groups
- Critical-thinking skills
- Culminating projects
- Cultural literacy
- Culturally responsive teaching
- Curriculum audits
- Curriculum mapping
- Cyber schools
- Data-based decision making
- Data-driven instruction
- Decentralization
- Deeper learning approach
- Desegregating schools
- Design thinking
- Differentiated instruction
- Digital citizenship
- Digital divide
- Digital learning
- Digital literacy
- Direct instruction
- Discipline gap
- Distance learning
- Distributed leadership
- Dropout prevention
- Dual-language learning
- e-learning
- Early childhood education
- Ecology education
- Edcamps
- Effective schools movement
- Emerging technologies (artificial intelligence, augmented reality, robotics, virtual reality)
- Emotional intelligence
- Empowering students
- EngageNY
- English as a second language immersion
- English language learning
- Equity education
- Every Student Succeeds Act
- Experiential learning
- Flipped classrooms
- Formative assessment
- Full-service schools
- Gamification
- Gates Foundation initiatives
- Gender gap
- Gender studies
- Gifted education
- Global education
- Global/financial literacy
- Google Docs
- Grade-level configurations (return to K–8 schools)
- Habits of Mind
- Harlem Children's Zone
- High School Late Start
- High-stakes testing
- Higher-order thinking skills
- Highly qualified teachers
- Homeschooling
- Inclusion
- Individualized education plans

- Individualized instruction
- Individuals with Disabilities Education Improvement Act
- Inquiry learning
- Instructional coaching
- Instructional leadership
- Instructional rounds
- International Baccalaureate
- International comparisons
- Job-embedded professional development
- Khan Academy
- Knowledge Is Power Program
- Learning management systems
- Learning styles
- Learning targets
- Lesson study
- LGBTQ advocacy groups
- LGBTQ education
- Magnet schools
- Maker movement
- Management by objectives
- Market-driven solutions
- Massive open online courses
- Mastery learning
- Merit pay
- Mindfulness learning
- Minecraft
- Mobile devices
- Multicultural education
- Multiple intelligences
- *A Nation at Risk*
- National Assessment of Educational Progress test
- National Board certification
- National Council of Teachers of Mathematics standards
- Next Generation Science Standards
- No Child Left Behind
- Online learning
- Online professional development
- Open education resources
- Open Source Schools
- Open-concept classrooms
- Opportunity gap
- Outdoor education
- Paideia
- Parent involvement
- Pathways to learning
- Pedagogy of the oppressed
- Peer coaching
- Peer tutoring
- Performance assessment
- Personal learning networks
- Portfolio assessment
- Positive behavioral intervention and support
- Poverty intervention programs
- Principal standards (ISLLC, Wallace Foundation)
- Privatization
- Problem-based learning
- Professional learning communities
- Proficiency-based education
- Programme for International Student Assessment
- Quality schools

- Race to the Top
- Reading First
- Reading Recovery
- Research-based teacher quality initiatives
- Response to Intervention
- Restorative justice
- Restructuring schools
- Rubrics
- Running start
- Safe schools
- Same-sex schools
- School choice
- School improvement plans
- School receivership
- School reform movement
- School to work
- Second language learning
- Senior culminating projects
- Servant leadership
- Service learning
- Site-based management
- Six traits of writing plus one
- Small schools movement
- Social justice
- Social networking
- Social-emotional learning
- Socratic seminars
- Standards movement
- Standards-based grading
- Standards-based reform
- Statewide testing
- STEM, STEAM, and STREAM
- Strategic planning
- Student voice

- Success for All
- Sustainable living education
- Teach for America
- Teacher frameworks
- Teacher leaders
- Teaching Channel
- Teaching with a growth mindset
- Teaching with tablets
- Team teaching
- Technology education
- Total quality management
- Transformative schools
- Trends in International Math and Science Study
- Turnaround schools
- Unconference
- Understanding by Design
- Universal Design for Learning
- Value-added measures
- Virtual academics
- Voucher movement
- Walk-throughs
- Web-based learning and collaboration
- Whole Child approach
- Whole school reforms
- Working on the Work
- Wraparound schools
- Writing across the curriculum
- Year-round schooling
- Zero tolerance
- 21st century schooling
- What should be added?

Appendix D: Perennial and Recent Education-Related Either/Or Dilemmas

Examine the either/or dilemmas and consider how students could benefit from paired topics if the outstanding features are integrated.

- 21st century skills versus content
- Academic press versus social support
- Academic programs versus career technical education
- Asset-based instruction versus deficit-based instruction
- Bilingual (or ESL) education versus English immersion
- Brick-and-mortar schools versus virtual schools
- Constructivism versus behaviorism
- Curriculum depth versus curriculum breadth
- Curriculum integration versus separate disciplines
- Equality versus excellence
- Formative assessment versus summative assessment
- Full-service community schools versus traditional schools
- General school population needs versus targeted student needs
- History versus social studies
- Homogeneous groups versus heterogeneous groups
- Informational/expository reading and writing versus literary/creative reading and writing
- Learning science (texts, lectures) versus doing science (labs, field trips)

- Lecture versus cooperative learning
- Liberal arts versus specialization and professional programs
- Local control versus state or federal control
- Multiage classes versus age/grade classes
- Nurture versus nature
- Phonics versus whole language
- Process versus product
- Public schools versus public- or foundation-supported charter schools
- Romanticism versus realism
- Student-centered teaching versus subject-centered teaching
- Traditional assessment versus alternative assessment
- Traditional math versus reform math
- What should be added?

Appendix E: The 15 Principles to Support Reforms of Substance

Principle #1: If a reformer or vendor tells you, "All the research supports 'New Reform X,' and the reform will be easy to implement in your school or classroom," it's time to head for the hills.

Principle #2: There is a difference between holding beliefs with humility and arrogance. Humility embraces feedback and growth; arrogance embraces neither.

Principle #3: Hear and celebrate the diverse voices in the community, then pause, before speaking your mind.

Principle #4: Today's quick fix is tomorrow's problem.

Principle #5: When making decisions about resources, programs, and professional development, always ask: How will this decision affect student learning and teacher success?

Principle #6: Successful implementation depends on wise insights and directions from the bottom, then support from the top.

Principle #7: Change that matters takes place in classrooms.

Principle #8: When you fall in love with a reform initiative, move it from the *heart* to the *head*. Then ask, Is this reform a shiny object, or will it affect student learning beyond today?

Principle #9: Publicly affirm and share the school mission because when frustrations capture the day, it is the anchor reminding everyone that education is sacred.

Principle #10: Proponents of proposed reforms should enthusiastically share the reform's "ancestry"; failing to do so should immediately raise credibility issues.

Principle #11: Embracing and synthesizing contrary ideas is challenging, but it reminds us that complexity and paradox are part of life.

Principle #12: Schools are not factories, and students are not merchandise.

Principle #13: To level the equity playing field, underserved students must be empowered and given voice to succeed in school and beyond.

Principle #14: When a diverse group of individuals engage in thoughtful collaboration, and know that what they say and do is valued, then actions to improve schools can become a moral enterprise.

Principle #15: Implementing reforms begins with building relationships.

References

Alexander, M. (2012). *The new Jim Crow*. New York: The New Press.

Alvy, H. B. (1996). Proceed with caution when adopting school reforms. *The International Educator, 10*(2), 1, 22.

Alvy, H. B. (2005). Preventing the loss of wisdom in schools: Respecting and retaining successful veteran teachers. *Phi Delta Kappan, 86*(10), 764–766, 771.

Alvy, H. B., & Robbins, P. (1998). *If I only knew. . . . : Success strategies for navigating the principalship*. Thousand Oaks, CA: Corwin.

Alvy, H. B., & Robbins, P. (2010). *Learning from Lincoln: Leadership practices for school success*. Alexandria, VA: ASCD.

American Educational Research Association. (2015). AERA statement on use of value-added models (VAM) for the evaluation of educators and education preparation programs. *Educational Researcher, 44*(8), 448–452.

American Statistical Association. (2014, April 8). *ASA statement on using value-added models for educational assessment*. Alexandria, VA: Author.

ASCD. (2015a, December). Elementary and Secondary Education Act: Comparison of the No Child Left Behind to the Every Student Succeeds Act. *Educator Advocates*. Retrieved from http://www.ascd.org/ASCD/pdf/siteASCD/policy/ESEA_NCLB_ComparisonChart_2015.pdf

ASCD. (2015b). Demographics do not equal destiny. *Education Update, 57*(8), 15.

ASCD. (2015c, May). Poverty and education. Policy points. *Educator Advocates*. Retrieved from http://www.ascd.org/ASCD/pdf/siteASCD/publications/policy points/Poverty-and-Education-May-15.pdf

ASCD. (2015d, February). *ASCD testing and accountability statement*. Retrieved from http://www.ascd.org/moratorium

ASCD. (n.d.). *Whole child.* Retrieved from http://www.ascd.org/whole-child.aspx

Ballantine, J., & Spade, J. (2004). *Schools and society: A sociological approach to education* (2nd ed.). Belmont, CA: Thomson-Wadsworth.

Benson, J. (2015). *Ten steps to managing change in schools: How do we take initiatives from goals to actions?* Alexandria, VA: ASCD.

Berliner, D., & Glass, G. (2014a). Chipping away: Reforms that don't make a difference. *Educational Leadership, 71*(9), 28–33.

Berliner, D., & Glass, G. (2014b). *Fifty myths and lies that threaten America's public schools: The real crisis in education.* New York: Teachers College Press.

Berliner, D., & Glass, G. (2015, February). Trust but verify. *Educational Leadership, 72*(5), 10–14.

Berman, P., & McLaughlin, M. (1978). *Federal programs supporting educational change, Vol. 8: Implementing and sustaining innovation.* Santa Monica, CA: RAND.

Best, J. (2006). Ten questions about fads. *Messenger, 14*(3). Retrieved from http://www1.udel.edu/PR/Messenger/05/03/ten.html

Bevan, B., Petrich, M., & Wilkinson, K. (2014, December/2015, January). Tinkering is serious play. *Educational Leadership, 72*(4), 28–33.

Blumenreich, M., & Jaffe-Walter, R. (2015, September). Social media illuminates some truths about school reform. *Phi Delta Kappan, 97*(1), 25–28.

Bransford, J., Brown, A., & Cocking, R. (Eds.). (2000). *How people learn: Brain, mind, experience, and school.* Washington, DC: National Academy Press.

Broader, Bolder Approach to Education. (2016, February 16). *A broader, bolder education policy framework.* Retrieved from http://www.boldapproach.org

Brooks, D. (2015). *The road to character.* New York: Random House.

Brown, J., & Isaacs, D. (2005). *The world café.* San Francisco: Berrett-Koehlar.

Bryk, A. (2015, December). 2014 AERA distinguished lecture: Accelerating how we learn to improve. *Educational Researcher, 44*(9), 467–477.

Bryk, A., & Schneider, B. (2002). *Trust in schools: A core resource for improvement.* New York: Russell Sage Foundation.

Busteed, B. (2014, October 1). Show students you care: It makes a difference. *Education Week, 34*(6), 26, 32.

Calfee, R. (2014). Knowledge, evidence, and faith. In K. Goodman, R. Calfee, & Y. Goodman (Eds.), *Whose knowledge counts in government literacy policy? Why expertise matters* (pp. 1–7). New York: Routledge.

Calvo, N., & Miles, K. (2011, December/2012, January). Turning crisis into opportunity. *Educational Leadership, 69*(4), 19–23.

Camera, L. (2014, December 10). Teachers chafe as Tennessee backtracks on Common Core. *Education Week, 34*(14), 16–17.

Carter, G. (2014, April). Creating solutions to the right questions. *Education Update, 56*(4), 8.

Cavanagh, S. (2014a, April 21). New standards sway purchasing plans. *Education Week, 33*(29). Retrieved from http://www.edweek.org/ew/articles/2014/04/23/29cc-business.h33.html?print=1

Cavanagh, S. (2014b, December 3). Tech vendors cloudy on K–12 buying needs. *Education Week, 34*(13), 14.

Cheney, L. V. (1994, October 20). The end of history. *Wall Street Journal.* Retrieved from http://online.wsj.com/media/EndofHistory.pdf

Cohen, M. (2013, May 24). *New School of New York graduation remarks.* New York.

Colangelo, L. (2015, July 14). Bronx teacher uses gardening to inspire students to study science. *New York Daily News.* Retrieved from http://www.nydailynews.com/new-york/education/bronx-teacher-gardening-change-lives-students-article-1.2292369

Collins, J. (2005). *Good to great and the social sectors.* New York: Harper Collins.

Collins, J., & Porras, J. (2002). *Built to last.* New York: Harper Business Essentials.

Comer, J. (n.d.). *How it works*. New Haven, CT: Comer School Development Program, Child Study Center, Yale School of Medicine. Retrieved from http://medicine.yale.edu/childstudy/comer

Committee of Ten. (1894). *Report of the Committee of Ten on secondary school studies*. New York: National Education Association.

Cuban, L. (2011). What schools can do in a democratic society. In R. Elmore (Ed.), *I used to think . . . and now I think . . .* (pp. 25–31). Cambridge, MA: Harvard Education Press.

Cuban, L. (2013). *Inside the black box of classroom practice*. Cambridge , MA: Harvard Education Press.

Daccord, T., & Reich, J. (2015, May). How to transform teaching with tablets. *Educational Leadership, 72*(8), 18–23.

Danielson, C. (2012, February, 15). An evaluation architect says teaching is hard, but assessing it shouldn't be. *New York Times SchoolBook*. Retrieved from http://www.wnyc.org/story/301604-an-evaluation-architect-says-teaching-is-hard-but-assessing-it-shouldnt-be/

Darling-Hammond, L. (2010). *The flat world and education*. New York: Teachers College Press.

Darling-Hammond, L. (2014, December/2015, January). Want to close the achievement gap? Close the teaching gap. *American Educator, 38*(4), 14–18.

Darling-Hammond, L., & Rothman, R. (2015). *Teaching in the flat world: Learning from high-performing systems*. New York: Teachers College Press.

David, J. (2011, March). High-stakes testing narrows the curriculum. *Educational Leadership, 68*(6), 78–80.

Davis, S. (2007, April). Bridging the gap between research and practice: What's good, what's bad, and how can one be sure? *Phi Delta Kappan, 88*(8), 569–578.

deMarrais, K. B., & LeCompte, M. (1999). *The way schools work: A sociological analysis of education*. New York: Addison Wesley Longman.

Duckworth, A. (2016, March 26). Don't grade schools on grit. *New York Times*. Retrieved from https://www.nytimes.com/2016/03/27/opinion/sunday/dont-grade-schools-on-grit.html

DuFour, R. (2004, May). What is a PLC? *Educational Leadership, 61*(8), 6–11.

DuFour, R., DuFour, R., & Eaker, R. (2008). *Revisiting professional learning communities at work*. Bloomington, IN: Solution Tree.

Dweck, C. (2008). *Mindset: The new psychology of success*. New York: Ballantine Books.

Easton, L. (2009, February/March). Protocols: A facilitator's best friend. *Tools for Schools, 12*(3), 1–8.

Elmore, R. (1995, December). Structural reform and educational practice. *Educational Researcher, 24*(9), 23–26.

Elmore, R. (1996). Getting to scale with good educational practice. *Harvard Educational Review, 66*(1), 1–26.

Elmore, R. (2010). Leading the instructional core: An interview with Richard Elmore. *In Conversation, 2*(3), 1–12.

Elmore, R. (2011). Policy is the problem and other hard-won insights. In R. Elmore (Ed.), *I used to think . . . and now I think. . . .* Cambridge, MA: Harvard University Press.

Epstein, J. (2007). Connections count. *Principal Leadership, 8*(2), 16–21.

Ferguson, M. (2013, December/2014, January). Failure is an option. *Phi Delta Kappan, 95*(4), 68–69.

Ferrero, D. (2011, March). The humanities: Why such a hard sell? *Educational Leadership, 68*(6), 22–26.

Ferriter, W., & Provenzano, N. (2013, November). Today's lesson: Self-directed learning for teachers. *Phi Delta Kappan, 95*(3), 16–21.

Flanigan, R. (2013, April 24). Vetting product research to determine what works. *Education Week, 32*(29), S10–S12.

Freire, P. (2000). *Pedagogy of the oppressed.* New York: Continuum.

Frontier, T., & Rickabaugh, J. (2014). *Five levers to improve learning: How to prioritize for powerful learning.* Alexandria, VA: ASCD.

Fullan, M. (2007). *The new meaning of educational change* (4th ed.). New York: Teachers College Press.

Fullan, M. (2011, May). *Choosing the wrong drivers for whole system reform.* (Seminar Series Paper No. 204). East Melbourne, Victoria, Australia: Center for Strategic Education.

Furman, G. (2012, January). Social justice leadership as praxis: Developing capacities through preparation programs. *Educational Administration Quarterly, 48*(2), 191–229.

Gabriel, R. (2016, May). The evolution of quality teaching and four questions for change. *Phi Delta Kappan, 97*(8), 50–53.

Gardner, H. (2011). From progressive education to educational pluralism. In R. Elmore (Ed.), *I used to think . . . and now I think. . . .* (pp. 41–48). Cambridge, MA: Harvard Education Press.

Gassenheimer, C. (2013, November). Let the practitioners do it. *Phi Delta Kappan, 95*(3), 39–42.

Gawande, A. (2010). *The checklist manifesto: How to get things right.* New York: Picador.

George, B. (2007). *True north: Discover your authentic leadership.* San Francisco: Jossey-Bass.

Gewertz, C. (2016, March 23). State solidarity erodes on standards testing. *Education Week, 35*(25), 1, 10–11.

Goodman, J. (1995). Change without difference: School restructuring in historical perspective. *Harvard Educational Review, 65*(1), 1–29.

Goodwin, B. (2015, June). Getting unstuck. *Educational Leadership, 72,* 8–12.

Goodwin, D. K. (2013). *The bully pulpit.* New York: Simon & Schuster.

Grubb, W. (2009, December/2010, January). Correcting the money myth. *Phi Delta Kappan, 91*(4), 51–55.

Hannah-Jones, N. (2016, July 31). The problem we all live with: Episode 562. *This American Life* [Radio Show]. New York: WBEZ.

Hanson, E. M. (2003). *Educational administration and organizational behavior* (5th ed.). Boston: Allyn & Bacon.

Hass, E., Fischman, G., & Brewer, J. (2014). *Dumb ideas won't create smart kids.* New York: Teachers College Press.

Hatch, T. (2013, November). Innovation at the core. *Phi Delta Kappan, 95*(3), 34–37.

Hattie, J. (2009). *Visible learning: A synthesis of over 800 meta-analyses related to achievement.* New York: Routledge.

Hattie, J. (2015, February). High-impact leadership. *Educational Leadership, 72*(5), 36–40.

Henke, L. (2011, May). Connecting with parents at home. *Educational Leadership, 68*(8), 38–41.

Herman, M. (2015, June 6). District smooths 1-to-1 initiative by heeding others' mistakes. *Education Week, 34*(35), 18–19.

Hernández, J. (2014, June 14). Common Core, in 9-year-old eyes. *New York Times.* Retrieved from https://www.nytimes.com/2014/06/15/education/common-core-in-9-year-old-eyes.html

Hernández, J., & Gebeloff, R. (2013, August 7). Test scores sink as New York adopts tougher benchmarks. *New York Times.* Retrieved from http://www.nytimes.com/2013/08/08/nyregion/under-new-standards-students-see-sharp-decline-in-test-scores.html

Herold, B. (2014a, March 28). Khan Academy lessons linked to Common Core standards. *Education Week, 33*(27), 1, 14.

Herold, B. (2014b, June 30). Popular 'maker movement' incompatible with Common Core, author contends. *Education Week.* Retrieved from http://blogs.edweek.org/edweek/DigitalEducation/2014/06/popular_maker_movement_incompa.html

Herold, B. (2014c, September 10). Hard lessons learned in L.A. iPad initiative. *Education Week, 34*(3), 1, 13.

Herold, B. (2015a, April). Districts weigh control over software buying. *Educational Week, 34*(27), S8.

Herold, B. (2015b, April 13). District allows schools to take lead on buying. *Education Week, 34*(27), S10.

Herold, B. (2015c, June 10). Why ed tech is not transforming how teachers teach. *Education Week, 34*(35), 8, 10, 12, 14.

Herold, B. (2016, February 3). PARCC scores lower for students who took exams on computers. *Education Week, 35*(20), 1, 11.

Herold, B., & Molnar, M. (2014, March 3). Research questions Common Core claims by publisher. *Education Week, 33*(23), 1, 12–13.

Hess, F., & McShane, M. (Eds.). (2014). *Common core meets educational reform.* New York: Teachers College Press.

Hill, L., Brandeau, G., Truelove, E., & Lineback, K. (2014, June). Collective genius. *Harvard Business Review, 92*(6), 94–102. Retrieved from http://hbr.org/2014/06/collective-genius

Hirsch, J. (2010). *Willie Mays: The life, the legend.* New York: Scribner.

Hord, S. M., Rutherford, W. L., Huling-Austin, L., & Hall, G. E. (1987). *Taking charge of change.* Alexandria, VA: ASCD.

IES. (2016, October 17). *Public high school graduation rate reaches new high, but gaps persist.* Retrieved from http://ies.ed.gov/whatsnew/pressreleases/10_17_2016.asp

Isaacson, W. (2011). *Steve Jobs.* New York: Simon & Schuster.

Jennifer, J., & Bearak, J. (2014). Teaching to the test in the NCLB era: How test predictability affects our understanding of student performance. *Educational Researcher, 43*(8), 381–389.

Jennings, J. (2015, April). ESEA at 50. *Phi Delta Kappan, 97*(7), 41–46.

Jochim, A. (2014). A reform at risk? The political realities. In F. Hess & M. McShane (Eds.), *Common Core meets educational reform.* New York: Teachers College Press.

Johnson, D. (2015, May). Power up: Choosing the right devices. *Educational Leadership, 72*(8), 82–83.

Johnson, J. (2013, April). The human factor. *Educational Leadership, 70*(7), 17–21.

Johnson, S. M. (2012). Having it both ways: Building the capacity of individual teachers and their schools. *Harvard Educational Review, 82*(1), 107–122, 167.

Johnson, S. M., Kraft, M., & Papay, J. (2011, June 29). *How context matters in high-need schools: The effects of teachers' working conditions on their professional satisfaction and their students' achievement.* (Project on the Next Generation of Teachers.) Cambridge, MA: Harvard Graduate School of Education.

Johnston, R. (2001, March 7). Central office is critical bridge to help schools. *Education Week, 20*(25), 1, 18–19.

Kahneman, D., Lovallo, D., & Sibony, O. (2011, June). The big idea: Before you make that big decision. *Harvard Business Review, 89*(6), 50–60.

Kanter, R. M. (1997). *On the frontiers of management.* Boston: Harvard Business School Press.

Kilpatrick, W. H. (1918, September). The project method: The use of the purposeful act in the educative process. *Teachers College Record, 19*, 319–334.

Klein, A., & Sparks, S. (2016, March 23). Getting to know i3. *Education Week, 35*(25), 12.

Kraft, M., Marinell, W., & Yee, D. (2016, March). *School organizational contexts, teacher turnover, and student achievement: Evidence from panel data* [Working Paper]. New York: The Research Alliance for NYC Schools.

Kuhn, J. (2014). *Fear and learning in America.* New York: William Morrow.

Kuhn, T. (1996). *The structure of scientific revolutions* (3rd ed.). Chicago: University of Chicago Press.

Ladd, H., Noguera, P., Reville, P., & Starr, J. (2016, May 11). Education policy should address student poverty. *Education Week, 35*(30), 22–23.

Leana, C. (2011). The missing link in school reform. *Stanford Social Innovation Review, 9*(4), 30–35.

Levitt, S., & Dubner, S. (2014). *Think like a freak.* New York: William Morrow.

Levy, H. (2016, April 13). How should schools purchase technology for the classroom? *Education Week, 35*(27), 23.

Lewis, K., & Burd-Sharps, S. (2016, May). *High school graduation in New York City: Is neighborhood still destiny?* Brooklyn, NY: Measure of America of the Social Science Research Council. Retrieved from http://ssrc-static.s3.amazonaws.com/wp-content/uploads/2016/04/27121634/MOA_HS_Brief.pdf

Madani, R., & Neudorf, D. (2015, October 31). Bandwagons: Jumping on and jumping off: How school leaders navigate a landscape of new frameworks and programs. Speech at EARCOS Conference, Bangkok, Thailand.

Martin, P., & Pines, S. (2015). *Improving ed-tech purchasing.* Washington, DC: Digital Promise. Retrieved from http://digitalpromise.org/wp-content/uploads/2014/11/Improving_Ed-Tech_Purchasing.pdf

Marx, G. (2014). *21 Trends for the 21st century.* Bethesda, MD: Education Week Press.

McChrystal, S. (2015). *Team of teams: New rules for engagement for a complex world.* New York: Portfolio/Penguin.

McDonald, J., Mohr, N., Dichter, A., & McDonald, E. (2013). *The power of protocols: An educator's guide to better practice* (3rd ed.). New York: Teachers College Press.

McGill, M. V. (2014, March 5). When education is but a test score. *Education Week, 33*(23), 20–21, 23. Retrieved from http://www.edweek.org/ew/articles/2014/03/05/23mcgill.h33.html

McGill-Franzen, A. (2010, May). The National Early Literacy Panel report: Summary, commentary, and reflections on policy and practices to improve children's early literacy. *Educational Researcher, 39*(4), 275–278.

McGregor, D. (1960). *The human side of enterprise.* New York: McGraw-Hill.

McGuinn, P. (2015, September). Complicated politics to the core. *Phi Delta Kappan,* *97*(1), 14–19.

McKibben, S. (2015, May). Five ways to support diverse families. *Education Update,* *57*(5), 1–5.

McKibben, S. (2016, May). Homing in on family relationships. *Education Update,* *58*(5), 2–3, 6–7.

Mehta, J. (2015). Escaping the shadow: *A Nation at Risk* and its far-reaching influence. *American Educator, 39*(2), 20–26.

Merrow, J. (2013, April 11). Michelle Rhee's reign of error. *Taking Note: Thoughts on Education from John Merrow* [Blog]. Retrieved from http://takingnote. learningmatters.tv/?p=6232

Meyer, P. (2014). The history of history standards: The prospects for standards for social studies. In F. Hess & M. McShane (Eds.), *Common Core meets educational reform* (pp. 118–139). New York: Teachers College Press.

Mitchell, G. (2015, June 8). Interview with Ambassador George Mitchell. *The Charlie Rose Show* [TV Show]. Arlington, VA: PBS.

Mondale, S., & Patton, S. (2001). *School: The story of American public education.* Boston: Beacon Press.

Moran, C., & Young, C. (2015, October). Questions to consider before flipping. *Phi Delta Kappan, 97*(2), 42–46.

Morena, C., Luria, C., & Mojkowski, C. (November, 2013). The latest twist on spreading innovation: One school at a time. *Phi Delta Kappan, 93*(3), 8–11.

Munson, L. (2011, March). What students really need to learn. *Educational Leadership, 68*(6), 10–14.

National Policy Board for Educational Administration (NPBEA). (2015). *Professional standards for educational leaders 2015.* Reston, VA: Author.

Nehring, J. (2007, February). Conspiracy theory: Lessons for leaders from two centuries of school reform. *Phi Delta Kappan, 88*(6), 425–432.

Newmann, F., & Wehlage, G. (1995). *Successful school restructuring.* Madison, WI: University of Wisconsin.

Nieto, S. (2011). Critical hope, in spite of it all. In R. Elmore (Ed.), *I used to think... and now I think....* (pp. 127–133) .Cambridge, MA: Harvard Education Press.

Noguera, P. (2011a, July 7). Reforms driven by education fads. *New York Times.* Retrieved from http://www.nytimes.com/roomfordebate/2011/03/06/why-blame-the-teachers/reforms-driven-by-education-fads

Noguera, P. (2011b, November). A broader and bolder approach. *Phi Delta Kappan, 93*(3), 8–13.

Office of Inspector General. (2006, September). *Final inspection report: The Reading First Program's grant application process.* (ED-OIG/133-F0017). Washington, DC: United States Department of Education.

O'Keeffe, J. (2012, April). In praise of isolation. *Phi Delta Kappan, 93*(7), 56–58.

Papay, J., & Kraft, M. (2016, May). The myth of the performance plateau. *Educational Leadership, 73*(8), 36–42.

Paul, R., & Elder, L. (2007). *A critical thinker's guide to educational fads.* Dillon Beach, CA: The Foundation for Critical Thinking Press.

Payne, C. M. (2008). *So much reform, so little change: The persistence of failure in urban schools.* Cambridge, MA: Harvard Education Press.

Peck, C., & Reitzug, U. (2012). How existing business management concepts became school leadership fashion. *Educational Administration Quarterly, 48*(2), 347–381.

Perkins, D., & Reese, J. (2014, May). Special topics: When change has legs. *Educational Leadership, 71*(8), 42–47.

Perkins-Gough, D. (2015, June). Rewriting the script in urban schools: A conversation with Yvette Jackson and Veronica McDermott. *Educational Leadership, 72*(9), 14–21.

Phillips, D. (2014). Research in the hard sciences, and in very hard "softer" domains. *Educational Researcher, 43*(1), 9–11.

Polikoff, M. (2015). How well aligned are textbooks to the Common Core standards in mathematics? *American Educational Research Journal, 52*(6), 1185–1211.

Popham, J. (2016, April). Standardized tests: Purpose is the point. *Educational Leadership, 73*(7), 44–49.

Pulliam, J., & Van Patten, J. (1999). *History of education in America* (7th ed.). New Jersey: Merrill, Prentice-Hall.

Ravitch, D. (2000). *Left back: A century of failed school reforms.* New York: Simon & Schuster.

Ravitch, D. (2010). *The death and life of the great American school system: How testing and choice are undermining American education.* New York: Basic Books.

Ravitch, D. (2013, August 7). It started with "No Child Left Behind." *New York Times.* Retrieved from http://www.nytimes.com/roomfordebate/2011/03/06/why-blame-the-teachers/it-started-with-no-child-left-behind

Ravitch, D. (2014). *Reign of error: The hoax of the privatization movement and the danger to America's public schools.* New York: Vintage Books.

Ravitch, D., Marchant, G., & David, K. (2014). The leader of the resistance: An interview with Diane Ravitch. *The Teacher Educator, 49*(3), 166–174.

Regan, M. D. (2016, November 20). What does voter turnout tell us about the 2016 election? *PBS NewsHour.* Retrieved from http://www.pbs.org/newshour/undates/voter.turnout-2016-elections/

Rice, C. (2010). *Extraordinary, ordinary people: A memoir of family.* New York: Random House.

Rickford, J., Wasow, T., Zwicky, A., & Buchstaller, I. (2007). Intensive and quotative all: Something old, something new. *American Speech, 82*(1), 3–31.

Riley, B. (2016, April). The value of knowing how students learn. *Phi Delta Kappan, 97*(7), 35–38.

Ripley, A. (2008, December 12). Can she save our schools? *Time, 172*(23), 36–44.

Robbins, P., & Alvy, H. (2014b). *The principal's companion: Strategies to lead schools for student and teacher success* (4th ed.). Thousand Oaks, CA: Corwin.

Robelen, E. (2013, May 15). Capacity issues confront implementation of standards. *Education Week, 32*(31), 1, 12–13.

Ronfeldt, M., Owens-Farmer, S., McQueen, K., & Grissom, J. (2015). Teacher collaboration in instructional teams and student achievement. *American Educational Research Journal, 52*(3), 475–514.

Rosenholtz, S. (1989). *Teachers' workplace.* New York: Longman.

Rothstein, R. (2008, April). Whose problem is poverty? *Educational Leadership, 65*(7), 8–13.

Russakoff, D. (2015a). *The prize: Who's in charge of America's schools?* New York: Houghton Mifflin Harcourt.

Russakoff, D. (2015b, September 21). Assessing the $100 million upheaval of Newark's public schools. *Fresh Air* [Radio Program]. Washington, DC: NPR. Retrieved from http://www.npr.org/2015/09/21/442183080/assessing-the-100-million-upheaval-of-newarks-public-schools

Rutledge, S., Cohen-Vogel, L., Osborne-Lampkin, L., & Roberts, R. (2015). Understanding effective high schools: Evidence for personalization for academic and social emotional learning. *American Educational Research Journal, 52*(6), 1060–1092.

Schmoker, M. (2010, September 29). When pedagogical fads trump priorities. *Education Week, 30*(5), 22–23.

Schmoker, M. (2011a). *Focus: Elevating the essentials to radically improve student learning.* Alexandria, VA: ASCD.

Schmoker, M. (2011b, November). Curriculum now. *Phi Delta Kappan, 93*(3), 70–71.

Schmoker, M. (2012, August 29). Why complex teacher evaluations don't work. *Education Week, 32*(2), 20, 24.

Schmoker, M. (2014, January 15). Education's crisis of complexity. *Education Week, 33*(17), 28.

Schmoker, M. (2015, October 21). Transforming P.D.: Beyond the mirage. *Education Week, 35*(9), 18–19.

Schreibman, L. (2005). *The science and fiction of autism.* Cambridge, MA: Harvard University Press.

Senge, P. (1992). *The fifth discipline.* London: Century Business.

Sirotnik, K. (1999, April). Making sense of educational renewal. *Phi Delta Kappan, 80*(8), 606–610.

Sparks, S. D. (2016a, March 24). Lessons from i3: California, Georgia schools learn from "failed" interventions. *Education Week.* Retrieved from http://blogs.edweek.org/edweek/inside-school-research/2016/03/stories_from_i3_california_sch.html

Sparks, S. D. (2016b, March 23). Federal i3: Giving wings to promising ideas, intervention targets 9th grade transition. *Education Week, 35*(25), 1, 12–13.

Sparks, S. D. (2016c, November 9). Education department awards $103 million in Investing in Innovation projects. *Education Week.* Retrieved from http://blogs.edweek.org/edweek/inside-school-research/2016/11/103_million_investing_in_innovation.html

Swanson, K. (2014, May). Edcamp: Teachers take back professional development. *Educational Leadership, 71*(8), 36–40.

Taylor, K. (2015a, November 25). Cuomo, in shift, is said to back reducing test scores' role in teacher reviews. *New York Times.* Retrieved from https://www.nytimes.com/2015/11/26/nyregion/cuomo-in-shift-is-said-to-back-reducing-test-scores-role-in-teacher-reviews.html

Taylor, K. (2015b, December 15). New York regents vote to exclude state tests in teacher evaluation. *New York Times,* A29.

Turnali, K. (2015, May 10). What is design thinking? *Forbes.* Retrieved from http://www.forbes.com/sites/sap/2015/05/10/what-is-design-thinking/#15e728123c18

Tyack, D., & Cuban, L. (1995). *Tinkering toward utopia.* Cambridge, MA: Harvard University Press.

United States Department of Education. (1983, April). *A nation at risk: The imperative for educational reform.* Washington, DC: The National Commission on Excellence in Education.

United States Department of Education. (2015, December 15). *U.S. high school graduation rate hits new record high.* Washington, DC: Author.

Varlas, L. (2015, April). Writing a master plan. *Education Update, 57*(4), 1, 4–5.

Vyse, S. (2005). Where do fads come from? In J. Jacobson, R. Foxx, & J. Mulick (Eds.), *Controversial therapies for developmental disabilities* (pp. 3–17). Mahwah, NJ: Lawrence Erlbaum Associates.

Walsh, J. A., & Sattes, B. D. (2015). *Questioning for classroom discussion: Purposeful speaking, engaged listening, deep thinking.* Alexandria, VA: ASCD.

West, P. (1989, September 13). Planning for technology: Few matching dollars with foresight. *Education Week.* Retrieved from http://www.edweek.org/ew/articles/1989/09/13/09040038.ho9.html

Wieman, C. (2014). The similarities between research in education and research in the hard sciences. *Educational Researcher, 43*(1), 12–14.

Wiggins, G., & McTighe, J. (1998). *Understanding by Design.* Alexandria, VA: ASCD.

Zenger, J., & Folkman, J. (2002). *The extraordinary leader.* New York: McGraw-Hill.

Zernike, K. (2015, October 24). Obama administration calls for limits on testing in schools. *New York Times.* Retrieved from http://www.nytimes.com/2015/10/25/us/obama-administration-calls-for-limits-on-testing-in-schools.html

Index

The letter *f* following a page number denotes a figure.

achievement
    collaboration and, 43
    environmental factors in, 139–140
    social capital and, 39
    social-emotional learning and,
        44–45
    socioeconomics of, 139–140,
        149–151
achievement gap, 150
American Dream narrative, 23–24
Amnesia, Historical
    avoiding, checklist for, 135
    big ideas, 128*f*
    consequences of, 119–123
    defined, 128*f*, 189
    in a dialogue among three
        teachers, 164–176
    discussion protocols, 181–183
    drawbacks, 128*f*
    education reform and, 124–125
    essential questions, 128*f*
    examples of, 128*f*
    Guideline as antidote to, 14*f*, 128*f*
    the maker movement, 126–127
    questions to promote
        collaborative discussion, 189
    the recency illusion, 123–124

Amnesia, Historical (*continued*)
    relabeling, examples of, 123–124
    technology and, 125–126
anchoring, 28–29
arrogance, 18–19, 48, 96, 145–147
ASCD Whole Child approach, 44, 139,
    159–160
assessment
    Eyes Off the Prize and, 108–111
    high-stakes
        teacher-centered
            instruction and, 109
        Underserved,
            Championing and
            Empowering the,
            150–151
        unintended consequences
            of, 106
    nonacademic indicators, 106
    opting out of, 81–82, 111
    in the Schools Replicate Society
        narrative, 26
autonomy, teacher, 39

A Ballpoint Pen Can Herd Cats, 49
Barn Raising Communities, narrative of
    Schools as, 27–28, 179

beliefs
holding with humility vs.
arrogance, 18–19
information inconsistent with, 34
mental models shaping, 21–22
paradigms shaping, 20–21
bias, 28–30, 36
Broader, Bolder, Approach (BBA) to
education, 47, 157–158
Building Assets, Reducing Risks (BARR)
program, 96–98
The Business "Solution"
avoiding, checklist for, 161–162
background, 142–143
big ideas, 148*f*
defined, 148*f*, 190
in a dialogue among three
teachers, 164–176
discussion protocols, 181–183
drawbacks, 148*f*
essential questions, 148*f*
examples of, 141, 148*f*
fallacies of, 140–142
Guideline as antidote to, 14*f*, 148*f*
hybrid approach to, 143–145
the price of arrogance, 145–147
questions to promote
collaborative discussion, 190
Schools as Factories narrative,
24–25, 138–141, 142
systems thinking in, 141, 144–145
transformational vs. instructional
leadership, 147

caring, 45, 134
Chan, Priscilla, 48
change
creating a culture of built on
trust, 92–94
lessons about, 100
morality and, 90–91
structural, factors in popularity
of, 91–92
change process
ancillary benefits, 94–95
arrogance vs. humility in the, 96,
176–177
drivers essential to and inhibiting
the, 93–95
phases in the, 81
success of, factors in, 81

Change Process, Respecting the
advantages, 89*f*
big ideas, 89*f*
Building Assets, Reducing Risks
(BARR) program, 96–98
checklist for, 101
defined, 89*f*, 192
in a dialogue among three
teachers, 164–176
discussion protocols, 183–185
essential questions, 89*f*
examples of, 89*f*
Hord et al. on, 80–81
Miami-Dade's One-to-One
Computer Initiative, 98–100
questions to promote
collaborative discussion, 192
the skeptic's role, 95
The Checklist Manifesto (Gwande), 7
civics education, 133–134
classrooms, flipped, 106
collaboration. *See also* Learning Community, Building a Collaborative
achievement and, 43
autonomy vs., 39
in the Comer Process, 45–46
institutionalized, 39
limiting, 37
limiting bias, 36
in resource allocation, 70
Comer Process, 45–46, 157
Common Core State Standards (CCSS),
81–82
Common Core Technology Project,
74–75
community partnerships
ASCD Whole Child approach,
159–160
Benjamin Franklin-Montefiore
affiliation, 159
Broader, Bolder, Approach (BBA),
47, 157–159
in Building a Collaborative
Learning Community, 43–48
examples of, 66
feedback in, 177
importance of, 66–67
modeling democracy, 134
public advocacy, 160–161
confidence, pedagogy of, 153
confirmation bias, 28–29

conversation, 36
curriculum, rich and well-rounded, 132–133

Dalton Plan, 123–124
decision making
    anchoring in, 28–29
    in the Comer Process, 45–46
    conformation bias in, 28–29
    design thinking framework for, 73–74
democracy, modeling, 133–134
design thinking, 73–74
Dewey, John, 120–121, 122
dropouts, 150

edcamps, 38
educational initiatives, list of, 195–198
educational reform
    arrogance and, 48
    defined, 2–3
    effective
        evaluating, 33–34
        focuses for, 11
        piloting for, 90
        promoting, 12
    either/or dilemmas, 121, 129–130, 199–200
    enduring, 5
    Historical Amnesia and, 124–125
    historically, list of initiatives, 195–198
    implementing responsibly, 7–8
    overload, dangers of, 5–7
    personalization in, 11–12
    prioritizing initiatives, big ideas for, 13
    social-emotional learning and, 11–12
    successful, 90
educational reforms of substance, implementing. See also Implementation, Minimizing the Enormous Difficulty of
    barn raising communities, similarity of schools to, 179
    collaboration, importance of, 178–179
    complexity of teaching, importance of acknowledging, 177

educational reforms of substance, implementing (continued)
    humility in, 176–177
    leadership role in teacher retention, 177
    mission, remaining faithful to the, 179
    narratives, breaking away from personal and professional, 176
    principles supporting, 1, 18, 34, 54, 64, 80, 90, 105, 111, 122, 129, 140, 149, 164, 176, 201–202
    social capital, importance of, 178–179
    teaching and learning, positive effect as requirement, 178
    technology initiatives, 178
    underserved students, supporting, 177–178
    vision, remaining faithful to the, 179
Educational Resource Strategies (ERS), 67–68
egos, implementation and, 84
either/or dilemmas, 121, 129–130, 199–200
Emancipation Proclamation, 31
EngageME P.L.E.A.S.E. data management and digital content system, 88
environmental factors in achievement, 139–140
Every Student Succeeds Act (ESSA), 8, 30, 142, 157
Exploratorium, 126–127
Eyes Off the Prize
    assessment and, 108–111
    avoiding, checklist for, 116
    big ideas, 112f
    defined, 112f, 189
    in a dialogue among three teachers, 164–176
    discussion protocols, 181–183
    drawbacks, 112f
    essential questions, 112f
    examples of, 104, 112f
    goal displacement, 105–106
    Guideline as antidote to, 14f, 112f
    questions to promote collaborative discussion, 189
    standards, focusing on, 107
    technology and, 107–108

fads, 4, 12, 55
failure, 31
families. *See also* parent partnerships
    diverse, reaching out to and
        respecting, 155–157
    empowering, culturally
        responsive strategies for, 154
    welcoming with home visits,
        154–155
feedback
    in community partnerships, 177
    honest, importance of, 13
    humility vs. arrogance in, 18–19
Finland, 141, 150
fiscal resources. *See* Human, Fiscal, and
    Material Resources, Effective Use of

Genius of the AND, 121, 129–130
goal displacement, 105–106
Good Friday peace agreement, 34
graduation rates, 139–140
guidance counselors, 151–152

history standards, 86–87
home visits, 154–155
How People Learn (Bransford, Brown &
    Cocking), 9
Human, Fiscal, and Material Resources,
    Effective Use of
    advantages, 65*f*
    big ideas, 65*f*
    checklist for, 76
    decision-making guidelines, 73–74
    defined, 65*f*, 192
    in a dialogue among three
        teachers, 164–176
    discussion protocols, 183–185
    essential questions, 65*f*
    examples of, 65*f*
    fiscal resources, 67–68
    for professional development,
        68–69
    questions to promote
        collaborative discussion, 192
    relative value of, 64, 66–67
    resource allocation guidelines,
        69–73
    technology procurement, 74–75
human capital, 39
humility, 18–19, 96, 176–177
Hunter, Madeline, 131

ideas
    enduring, 4–5, 12, 13
    separating from the individual, 49
If I Only Knew . . . (Alvy & Robbins),
    92–93
Implementation, Minimizing the
    Enormous Difficulty of. *See also*
    educational reforms of substance,
    implementing
    avoiding, checklist for, 101
    big ideas, 89*f*
    defined, 89*f*, 188
    in a dialogue among three
        teachers, 164–176
    discussion protocols, 181–183
    drawbacks, 89*f*
    egos, effects of, 84
    essential questions, 89*f*
    examples of, 81–83, 86–88, 89*f*
    Guideline as antidote to, 14*f*, 89*f*
    mistakes, guidelines for avoiding,
        99
    organizational complexity and,
        83–84
    outside forces and, 84
    patience, importance of, 85–86
    questions to promote
        collaborative discussion, 188
    scaling up, 85
    time, importance of, 85–86
    unintended consequences of,
        83–84
    unpredictability factor, 83
innovation, 5, 13, 39
internet narrative trap, 20
Investing in Innovation Fund (i3) initia-
    tives, 87–88
IQ tests, 150, 151–152

job-alike sessions, 38–39

leadership
    role in teacher retention, 177
    transformational vs.
        instructional, 147
learning
    complexity of, 10–11, 178
    cooperative, 108
    focus for school reform, 11
    individualized, 123–124
    social-emotional, 11–12, 44–45, 106

Learning Community, Building a
   Collaborative
     advantages, 35*f*
     the BBA approach, 47
     benefits of, 34, 36, 42–43
     big ideas, 35*f*
     checklist for, 50
     the Comer Process, 45–46
     community partnerships in,
       43–48
     defined, 35*f*, 191
     in a dialogue among three
       teachers, 164–176
     discussion protocols, 183–185
     edcamps, 38
     essential questions, 35*f*
     examples, 35*f*
     in implementing reforms of
       substance, 178–179
     job-alike sessions, 38–39
     parent partnerships in, 43–46
     questions to promote
       collaborative discussion, 191
     relationships in, 44–45
     social capital in, 39–42
     trusting teacher voices, 36–37
     unconferences, 38
     virtual options, 37–38
Lincoln, Abraham, 30–31
literacy, 11, 62–64

maker movement, 120–121, 126–127
material resources. *See* Human, Fiscal,
   and Material Resources, Effective
   Use of
Mays, Willie, 41–42
mental models shaping beliefs, 21–22
Miami-Dade's One-to-One Computer
   Initiative, 98–100
mindset, fixed vs. growth, 27
mission, defined, 105
Mission and Vision, Sustaining a
   Coherent
     advantages, 112*f*
     big ideas, 112*f*
     checklist for, 116
     defined, 112*f*, 193
     in a dialogue among three
       teachers, 164–176
     discussion protocols, 183–185
     essential questions, 112*f*

Mission and Vision, Sustaining a
   Coherent (*continued*)
     examples of, 112*f*
     in implementing reforms of
       substance, 179
     public affirmation and sharing,
       111, 113
     questions to promote
       collaborative discussion, 193
     reassessing the mission, 113–114
     strategic planning and, 114
     technology implementation and,
       115
morality, change and, 90–91

narratives
   of animosity, resolving, 34
   personal, factors shaping, 19–20
   of realism, 22–23
   rejecting to move forward, 30–33
   of romanticism, 22–23
narratives in education, common
   the American Dream, 23–24
   No Excuses, 25–26, 139, 157
   Schools as Barn Raising
     Communities, 27–28, 177
   Schools as Factories, 24–25,
     138–141, 142
   Schools Replicate Society, 26–27
Narrative Trap
   avoiding, checklist for, 50
   bias in the, 28–30
   big ideas, 35*f*
   creating a, 18–19
   defined, 35*f*, 187
   in a dialogue among three
     teachers, 164–176
   digital, 20
   discussion protocols, 181–183
   drawbacks, 35*f*
   essential questions, 35*f*
   examples, 35*f*
   Guideline as antidote to, 14*f*, 35*f*
   questions to promote
     collaborative discussion, 187
   results of the, 19
*A Nation at Risk: The Imperative for
   Educational Reform (ANAR)*, 3, 9,
   21–22, 124
Nava, Henry, 151–152
Nava, Julian, 151–152

needs assessment in resource allocation, 71
Next Generation Science Standards (NGSS), 82
No Child Left Behind Act (NCLB), 8, 9, 30, 31–32, 106
No Excuses narrative, 25–26, 139, 157
Northern Ireland, 34

One-to-One Computer Initiative, Miami-Dade, 98–100
online resources, 72–73
open education resources (OERs), 72–73
opportunity gap, 66, 133, 139–140, 158
opt-out movement, 81–82, 111
organizational complexity, implementation and, 83–84
Overpromising
    catchphrases, 59–61
    marketing strategies, 59–61
    Reading First program example of, 62–64
    slogans, 59–61
    unintended consequences of, 57–58
    when research agendas marginalize context, 62
Overpromising/Overloading
    avoiding, checklist for, 76
    big ideas, 65*f*
    defined, 53, 65*f*, 188
    in a dialogue among three teachers, 164–176
    discussion protocols, 181–183
    drawbacks, 65*f*
    essential questions, 65*f*
    examples of, 54–57, 65*f*
    factors contributing to overloading, 58–59
    Guideline as antidote to, 14*f*, 65*f*
    questions to promote collaborative discussion, 188
    results of, 53–55

paradigm shifts, 20
paradigms shaping beliefs, 20–21
parent partnerships. *See also* families
    in Building a Collaborative Learning Community, 43–46
    the Comer Process, 45–46, 157

parent partnerships (*continued*)
    home visits for, 154–155
    modeling democracy, 134
parents, accommodating, 58
Parent Teacher Home Visits Project, 155
Parkhurst, Helen, 123–124
Partnership for Assessment of Readiness for College and Careers (PARCC), 81–82
partnerships. *See* community partnerships; parent partnerships
pedagogical capital, 43
Pedagogy of the Oppressed (Freire), 43–44
personalization, 11–12, 44–45, 123–124, 134
pluralism in education, 32–33
polar narratives, 18
poverty rate, U.S., 150
principals, standards for, 12
The Prize (Russakoff), 47
professional development, 24, 68–69, 72, 132
progressive education, 32–33, 120
project method, 120

questions, celebrating courageous, 13

Race to the Top, 9, 30, 32
Reading First program, 62–64
realism, narratives of, 22–23
recency illusion, 123–124
reformers, teachers vs., 17–18
relabeling, examples of, 123–124
relationships. *See also* community partnerships; parent partnerships
    achievement and, 44–45
    caring, 45, 134
    with families, creating, 154–157
    with vendors, 73, 75
research bias, 29–30
resource audits, 72. *See also* Human, Fiscal, and Material Resources, Effective Use of
return on investment (ROI), 70–71
romanticism, narratives of, 22–23

schools, virtual, 24–25
Schools as Barn Raising Communities narrative, 27–28, 177

Schools as Factories narrative, 24–25, 138–141, 142
Schools Replicate Society narrative, 26–27
scientific management, 24–25, 138–139, 142
Senge, Peter, 21, 83, 141, 144
social capital
    in Building a Collaborative Learning Community, 39–40
    collaboration in strengthening, 36
    in implementing reforms of substance, 178–179
    successful use of, 41–42
social-emotional learning, 11–12, 44–45, 106
social infrastructure focus of reform, 11
Society, narrative of Schools as Replicators of, 26–27
socioeconomics of achievement, 139–140, 149–151
solutionitis, 55
special education fads, 55
strengths, focusing on, 153–154
The Structure of Scientific Revolutions (Kuhn), 20
systems thinking, 83, 141, 144–145

Taking Charge of Change (Hord et al.), 80–81
teachers
    autonomy, 39
    reformers vs., 17–18
    retaining, leadership role in, 177
teaching
    complexity of, 10–11, 177
    culturally responsive strategies, 154–155
    in Finland, 141
    focus for school reform, 11
    improving, 132
    teacher-centered, 109
Teaching Practices, Embracing Timeless and Eclectic
    advantages, 128f, 130–131
    big ideas, 128f
    caring relationships, 134
    checklist for, 135
    curriculum, rich and well-rounded, 132–133
    defined, 128f, 193
    democracy, modeling, 133–134

Teaching Practices, Embracing Timeless and Eclectic (continued)
    in a dialogue among three teachers, 164–176
    discussion protocols, 183–185
    essential questions, 128f
    examples of, 128f
    Genius of the AND, 129–130
    lesson design, 131–132
    questions to promote collaborative discussion, 193
technology
    Miami-Dade's One-to-One Computer Initiative, 98–100
    planning for, 125–126
    supporting initiatives for educational reform, 178
    Sustaining a Coherent School Mission and Vision, 115
technology procurement, 74–75, 125–126
Theory X and Y, 92–93
total cost of ownership (TCO), 70–71
True North (George), 145

unconferences, 38
Underserved, Championing and Empowering the
    advantages, 148f
    ASCD Whole Child approach, 159–160
    big ideas, 148f
    Broader, Bolder, Approach (BBA) in, 157–159
    checklist for, 161–162
    community-school integration, 157–160
    defined, 148f, 194
    in a dialogue among three teachers, 164–176
    discussion protocols, 183–185
    equity, equality, and excellence, focusing on, 153
    essential questions, 148f
    examples of, 148f
    families, creating relationships with, 154–157
    implementing reforms of substance, 177–178
    the Nava story, 151–152
    need for, 149–151

Underserved, Championing and
    Empowering the (*continued*)
    public advocacy, 160–161
    questions to promote
        collaborative discussion, 194
    strength and growth approach,
        153–154
    wraparound initiatives, 159
Understanding by Design, 122
unpredictability factor in implementa-
    tion, 83

vendor relationships, 73, 75
virtual collaboration, 37–38
Visible Learning (Hattie), 9
vision, defined, 105. *See also* Mission and
    Vision, Sustaining a Coherent

Whole Child approach (ASCD), 44, 139,
    159–160
WriteUp! program, 88

Zuckerberg, Mark, 47–48

About the Author

Harvey Alvy served as a practicing principal for 14 years in both elementary and secondary schools. His teaching career began at the Frederick Douglass School in New York City, and he later taught in middle and high schools in the United States and abroad. Alvy's experience in multicultural international schools is extensive and includes serving the Singapore American School, The American International School in Israel, the American Embassy School in New Delhi, and the American School in Kinshasa. Alvy is a founding member of the Principals' Training Center for International Schools and was an NAESP National Distinguished Principal. He held the William C. Shreeve Endowed Professorship in Educational Administration at Eastern Washington University (EWU), where he now serves as a professor emeritus. In 2004, he received the EWU CenturyTel Faculty Achievement Award for Teaching Excellence.

Alvy earned a doctorate in educational administration from the University of Montana focusing on the problems of new principals.

He conducts presentations and workshops, both nationally and internationally, on the leadership of Abraham Lincoln, the new principal, instructional leadership, and distinguishing between fads and substance to promote school change. His publications include *Learning from Lincoln: Leadership Practices for School Success*, *The New Principal's Fieldbook: Strategies for Success*, *The Principal's Companion: Strategies for Making the Job Easier*, 4th edition, *If I Only Knew . . . : Success Strategies for Navigating the Principalship*, and in Mandarin, *The Principal Management Handbook: The American Principal's Approach to Successful Administration*. Alvy can be reached at halvy@ewu.edu.

Acknowledgments

The ideas in this book reflect my current thinking on educational fads and ideas of substance but have been shaped by a lifetime of engaging in conversations with individuals who have been part of my professional and personal life. I am grateful to everyone who has shared a powerful idea with me, challenged my thinking, or encouraged me to explore a research theory or practical concept that I would have otherwise overlooked. Most of all, I have been influenced by the personal examples of outstanding educators and friends who work each day to improve the experiences of students, teachers, parents, and community colleagues. My first principal at the Frederick Douglass School in Harlem, the late Dr. Lionel McMurren, helped a young teacher gain confidence; he gently mentored me when I needed it most. Other school leaders, teachers, secretaries, university colleagues, and students who have graciously influenced my work include Ted Coladarci, Forrest Broman, Elaine Levy, Drew Alexander, David Chojnacki, Jane Liu, Leonie Brickman, Rob Beck, Betty Bicksler, Don Bergman, Bob Gibson, Mike Dunn, Pat Wolfe, Les Portner, Billie Gehres, Sharon Jayne, Joan Dickerson, Jim Howard, Steve Smedley, Dick Krajczar, Becky Berg, Josh Garcia, Deb Clemens, Kathy Clayton, Tammy Campbell, Carole Meyer, Tara

Haskins, Vince Aleccia, Lynn Briggs, Alan Coelho, Chris Valeo, Chris Stewart, Jon Hammermeister, Bob Connor, Nili Sadovnik, Abby Chill, Sandy Bensky, Uma Maholtra, Claire Brusseau, Sonya Seth, Sonya Phillips, Christina Campbell, Nelson and Lisa File, Steve Kapner, Troy Heuett, Sean Dotson, Lori Wyborney, Mel Kellner, Konni deGoejj, the late Boni Rahaman, Dr. Harry Savage Sr., Tom Overholt, Bill Shreeve, Phil Snowden, and Len Foster. Family and friends who have encouraged me include Norman Alvy and Vicki Alvy ("You're the best!"), Paul Schmidt, Richard Shustrin, Alan Siegel, Ted Otto, Dick Donley, Casey and Chris Tuckerman, Ken and Ellen Karcinell, Jim and Sally Bogaert, John and Jan Mathews, Joel Goldberg ("If you have something to say, say it"), and Joe Sinclair.

Pam Robbins has been a wonderful professional colleague, mentor, and friend for more than 20 years—how our work depended on the wisdom of our mothers! Thanks to two Eastern Washington University colleagues who helped flesh out critical book ideas: Dr. Rick Phillips, drawing from his assessment work, stressed, "Context is everything"; and Dr. Marion Moore shared painful research on fads in special education.

Genny Ostertag, ASCD's Director of Content Acquisitions, helped shape this project from the beginning; her encouragement and timely advice were indispensable. Liz Wegner edited the book with skill and enthusiasm; her holistic grasp of important concepts made a difference. Genny and Liz, thank you.

When engaged in a major writing project I think often of my late parents Rebecca and Daniel Alvy—thanks mom and dad for encouraging me each day. Finally, I'm very fortunate that my two biggest supporters, my wife Bonnie and daughter Rebecca, are always there—even if it gets a little embarrassing at times! I am grateful for their love.